Leading
Women
Who
Wound

Leading Women Who Wound

Strategies for an Effective Ministry

Sue Edwards &
Kelley Mathews

MOODY PUBLISHERS

CHICAGO

Editor: Jocelyn Green
Interior Design: Ragont Design
Cover Design: Garborg Design Works, Inc., Savage, MN
Cover Photo: BigStockPhoto.com

Library of Congress Cataloging-in-Publication Data
Edwards, Sue
    Leading women who wound : strategies for an effective ministry / Sue Edwards & Kelley Mathews.
        p. cm.
    Includes bibliographical references.
    ISBN 978-0-8024-8153-5
    1. Church work with women. 2. Women in church work. 3. Women—Religious life. 4. Women—Psychology. I. Mathews, Kelley II. Title.

BV4445.E39 2009
259.082—dc22

                                                                    2008042240

We hope you enjoy this book from Moody Publishers. Our goal is to provide high-quality, thought-provoking books and products that connect truth to your real needs and challenges. For more information on other books and products written and produced from a biblical perspective, go to www.moodypublishers.com or write to:

Moody Publishers
820 N. LaSalle Boulevard
Chicago, IL 60610

1 3 5 7 9 10 8 6 4 2

Printed in the United States of America

CONTENTS

Acknowledgments

Debts of gratitude are the most difficult to collect and we owe that debt to many who helped with this book. When friends, family, or colleagues heard we were writing a book on women and conflict, many responded, "We desperately need that book! Let me tell you what happened to me . . . " Over coffee or lunch, they shared their experiences, lessons learned, regrets, and triumphs. We doctored their stories, weaving some together and dimming the details, but the essence remains intact. Thanks for your vulnerability and candor. We hope and pray that other women will learn from your mistakes and echo your victories as they train to become skilled peacemakers too.

Thanks to Steve Roese, executive pastor of Irving Bible Church, for your insight when working with leaders and particularly female ones, and for modeling how to create an ethos conducive to healthy conflict resolution. To Kelly Arabie and Lynn Quernemon for valuable comments on the first draft. To Jeanne Ballard, who helped us understand the special challenges for pastors' wives. And, of course, to our husbands David Edwards and John Mathews for your steady support and partnership. Your daily sacrifices made this project possible.

Finally, we are grateful to Moody Publishers, particularly Jennifer Lyell (Acquisition Editor, Women's Books), for believing in this project and giving us the opportunity to speak into the lives of women who need encouragement and practical skills as they labor for Jesus. Books on conflict for men are plentiful but books for women are scarce. May this book help fill that void and may the Lord bless those who helped make our dream a reality.

Authors' Note

The illustrations and stories in this book are based on true accounts. However, names, situations, and specifics have been altered to protect participants. We understand that these accounts are not "easy reading," especially for tenderhearted women. Some are extreme examples, atypical of every woman's experience. Nevertheless, many of the seasoned women we interviewed were quick to supply a serious story. Bear with us in the first few chapters as we set the stage for positive strategies and solutions to follow.

Introduction

Turn away from evil and do what is right!
Strive for peace and promote it!

—Psalm 34:14

"You are holding women's hands to hell," snapped Sylvia, glaring at Sue over the conference table. Both women were respected, experienced Bible teachers in the same church. Every week hundreds of women sat at their feet to learn about the joy, peace, and love of Jesus. But today these two leaders were embroiled in a conflict that threatened to destroy their reputations and ministries.

The executive pastor sat between them, attempting to negotiate. Sylvia charged Sue with false teaching. Her purpose was to discredit Sue and close down her rival class. What had Sue done to deserve this harsh rebuke? Had she declared that the Bible was unreliable? Had she taught women that Jesus was not divine? Had she encouraged women to pursue ungodly lifestyles? No. The charge was cheap grace. Sylvia believed that Sue taught women they were saved when they were not. She accused Sue of being soft on repentance and insisted that she be sacked. Most of the women in the church did not understand the accusation. Most scholars with different views on the issue respectfully agree to disagree. But not Sylvia.

The conflict had begun months earlier when Sylvia barged into Sue's class moments before Sue was slated to teach. She denounced Sue in front of several discussion group leaders and then stomped out. Sue was shaken but managed to pull herself together and teach her lesson. For weeks Sylvia harassed Sue by phoning her at home. She hired a stenographer to transcribe one of Sue's messages, created a booklet arguing for Sue's dismissal, and presented the document to the pastor.

The pastor's initial response was slow and indecisive. As a result, the conflict lasted more than a year with Sue ultimately exonerated but emotionally bruised. A bitter Sylvia eventually left the church. Attendance in both studies waned that year as word of the turmoil spread. Disillusioned women left the church or enrolled in other Bible studies.

LESSONS TO PASS ON

I am Sue and that ferocious assault on my integrity taught me many lessons. First, I was unprepared. No one ever told me to expect personal attacks and conflict when serving the Lord and Christians. Some weeks I worked fifty hours as a lay volunteer, and I expected the pastors to appreciate and protect me. I was naive. And I was ignorant. I had never been taught strategies to manage conflict, so I did not always respond wisely.

Second, in the crucible, I discovered personal weaknesses that surprised me. I learned that I was too concerned with what people thought of me. I was a people-pleaser. I was quick to run from conflict rather than face it head-on. I thought if I ignored the attacks, they would go away. I realized that well-meaning but unbalanced Christians can be mean-spirited in their zeal and can harm others.

I was almost one of their casualties. But with the help of wise women at my side, I survived—and thrived. The experience grew and seasoned me. I learned to hold up my head, take the high road day by day, and to perform for an audience of One. Over the years I have witnessed other conflicts and, while I would not describe these years as full of conflict, often—too often—quarrels have arisen. Most have been minor, but others, like the conflict with Sylvia, have threatened the life of the ministry. Yet in these disputes, with God's enabling strength and biblical strategies, I have learned to hammer out effective solutions, grow in my faith, and glorify Him in the process.

GENDER DIFFERENCES

Both men and women endure conflict, but men and women perceive and process conflict differently. There are many excellent books by men to help men navigate conflict and personal attacks, but female perspectives tailored for women are scarce. Women need direction on how to manage conflict with other *women*. How do we deal with our emotions through painful rejection caused when other women are insensitive, manipulating, or just plain mean? What does the Bible tell us? To be thoroughly equipped for conflict, we must understand and master strategies specifically related to conflict with other women. When we do, we can usually nip these skirmishes in the bud before they bloom.

IT'S MORE COMMON THAN YOU THINK

One member of a leadership team, which was formed to improve a particular ministry, didn't like some of the proposed changes and met secretly with the pastor, maligning the ministry. The leadership team felt betrayed, and the ministry was temporarily sidetracked.

A children's ministry planning committee could not agree on the next year's curriculum, expressing its foundational differences in constant, petty skirmishes. The next year, many of the leaders resigned.

During a small group meeting, discussion over one person's questionable theology escalated into an argument, while another member—in pain because of her parents' severe health problems and needing the love and support of her brothers and sisters—left the house in tears, her more pressing needs completely ignored.

In a church Bible class, two people embroiled in a theological discussion over the sovereignty of God and free will ended their debate by taking swings at each other. Imagine trying to explain that to visitors! These examples affected specific ministries within the church, but conflict also takes its toll on entire churches and congregations. Consider these statistics:

- 23 percent of all current pastors in the United States have been fired or forced to resign.[1]

- 25 percent of the churches in one survey reported conflict in the previous five years that was serious enough to have a lasting influence on congregational life.[2]

- Fifteen hundred pastors leave their assignments every month in the United States because of conflict, burnout, or moral failure.[3]

Although these statistics apply mostly to men, we all know that women are involved in many of these conflicts, and were undoubtedly the cause of some. Imagine the damage on ministries, personal lives, and God's reputation. These startling statistics should compel you to seek positive solutions so you won't become one. You can avert conflict in your life and ministry, but not without proactive intentionality!

CAUSES AND COMPLEXITY

Conflicts vary in complexity. Some are between Christians serving together. Others are between those who serve and those being served. At other times leaders cannot agree. Then there is friction between ministries within a church. Sometimes these disagreements are resolved graciously and the parties grow from the experience. But when the parties have not learned how to resolve conflict biblically, too often, it ends like Sue and Sylvia—in disaster! The wounded limp away, sometimes never to serve again. The world hears one more account of how Christians "just can't get along."

We are writing this book to prevent what happened to Sue from happening to you. Personal attacks, difficult people, and conflict are all inevitable in ministry. You won't be the exception! Whether you are volunteering a few hours a week or serve on full-time staff, you need to prepare yourself. These issues challenge everyone in ministry, especially as the rudeness so easily accepted by our culture is reflected in the church. Respect for authority has declined. People-bashing and name-calling are common. Watch the political sparring on the news or the congressional approval hearings. People with different perspectives routinely attack the integrity of their "adversary," and that practice has invaded ministry. We are not immune from the culture, and whether we volunteer in the children's ministry, help with youth, lead a Bible study, prepare meals in the church kitchen, or count the money, we will encounter people with similar attitudes. But in most cases, we can turn potential altercations into an opportunity to glorify God.

AN OVERVIEW OF THE BOOK

What do women need to know to arm themselves for personal attacks, conflict, and difficult people? First we need to know ourselves. Some of us are more vulnerable than others. We will explore personality traits and character issues that set us up for problems. We will work on ways to toughen up, snuff out people-pleasing, and practice peacemaking in our everyday lives and relationships. Peacemaking is a skill and we learn by practicing *before* we are in the middle of ministry conflict.

We will learn how to differentiate between a woman who is bringing helpful, constructive criticism from one who is out to harm us or our ministry. It is not always easy to tell, especially at first. Several women fooled me for years. But red flags can alert us to possible danger and keep us on guard. We can also take steps to avert conflict before it strikes.

If we do encounter a woman whose intentions are not honorable, we must know what to do. If she is well-intentioned and we handle it well, we may defuse the situation immediately and even win a friend. But we must know how to skillfully disarm women who wound.

Ultimately we must learn to love them. This may be one of the most difficult assignments Jesus will ever give us. But He instructed us to love those who hurt us, and He set the example. We will never learn to love them unless we draw on the Holy Spirit for supernatural enabling. This will test our faith and require complete dependence and surrender. Everything in us will want to lash out if we believe we are being treated unjustly. But it is possible to love those who attack us—in fact, it's mandatory if we are to thrive in the midst of conflict.

We will learn practical peacemaking skills to overcome our defensiveness. We will discover what it means to live out tough love. We must master wise strategies as we process with women who hurt us. The Bible gives us clear directives, and we will examine related passages carefully with an eye to how this looks in various situations. We will hear stories from women who looked to God for help and learn from their examples.

A good leader also prepares women around her for conflict and personal attacks. As leaders, what proactive steps can we take? What training can we provide to equip our teams? How can we spare women from what happened to Sue and Sylvia? We will examine training tools, conflict resolution covenants, and ideas that have worked for women leaders throughout the country.

We have included a chapter for male ministers. In our experience, if a ministry conflict between women escalates, male leaders are often asked to oversee the negotiation process. Their tendency is to ignore gender differences and expect women to act like men. Big mistake. Chapter Nine enumerates some of the differences and provides strategies that work with women.

Consider reading and discussing this book with friends, coworkers, or people you lead. We created questions at the end of each chapter to help groups process and apply the principles in this book. Interactive learning in community enriches the experience and improves retention.

A culture of peace provides many blessings *(James 3:18)*:

- Marriages, friendships, and other relationships are strengthened and preserved, resulting in fewer divorces and a lower turnover of members, staff, and volunteers.
- Members resolve most of their conflicts personally and privately, releasing pastors from the "complaint loop."
- Conflicts are turned into opportunities for people to be freed from sin and mature in faith and character.
- Ministries and missions are more united and fruitful.
- Peace and reconciliation reveal the health of your church, glorifying Jesus Christ, enhancing your witness, and stimulating church growth (Acts 2:47).

—Ken Sande, President, Peacemaker Ministries[4]

REWARDS AND BENEFITS

Usually with solid strategies, supernatural enabling, and wise leadership, conflict can be averted or resolved. Women can overcome their differences and become good friends—or at least avoid enmity, maintaining the unity of the body, peace among believers, and God's good name. But not always. Jesus had His Judas and, if you are in ministry for the long haul, you probably will too. If resolution is impossible, what then? You can still prevail. And God may have some powerful lessons to teach you as He takes you through the ordeal. These may be the tools He uses to strengthen you for the future. God promises to use all things for His glory and our good if we submit them to Him. I can testify and thank God for Sylvia and our year-long conflict, not because it was pleasant, but because God used it to season and strengthen me.

Our hope is to equip you as well for conflict that may be waiting. God has plans to use each of us to love and serve others. He has given us gifts, talents, and life experiences to prepare us. The Enemy often uses personal attacks and conflict to discourage us, hoping to make us a casualty of war, and to sidetrack us from God's plan for our lives. Don't let him!

If you picked up this book because you are in the midst of a battle, your emotions are probably in high gear and the felt need is real. May God use this book to bring honor to Him and help you each step of the way toward a godly resolution. If you are not in the midst of the battle, all the better. Proverbs 24:10 tells us that "If you faint in the day of trouble, your strength is small." The point is to build up your strength *before* the day of trouble. You build up your spiritual strength by gaining life skills to cope and conquer. Conflict awaits all of us who want to be women of influence for Jesus. It's best to prepare beforehand. Join us as we explore leading women who wound.

And the fruit that consists of righteousness is planted in peace among those who make peace.

—James 3:18

Expect Women Who Wound

My brothers and sisters, consider it nothing but joy when you
fall into all sorts of trials, because you know that the testing of your
faith produces endurance. And let endurance have its perfect effect,
so that you will be perfect and complete, not deficient in anything.

—James 1:2–5

"I just want to know what the Bible says," demanded Gail, a student in my women's weekly Bible class. As I (Sue) descended from the platform, she was on me, nose to nose. My back pressed to the wall, I felt silly in my costume, sprayed-on grey hair, and granny makeup. For seven weeks I lectured, pulling my main points straight from the text. But for the finale, I dressed the part of a character from a story and illustrated the message with a dramatic presentation. The women seemed to love the unique lesson, all except Gail.

Her tirade lasted several minutes but I don't remember specifics—just a tightness all over my body, a warmth that began small and then engulfed me in a wave of adrenaline and emotion. The room faded and I was left feeling alone and exposed. I wanted to slip away and hide, but a luscious lunch with small group leaders waited, a time to celebrate God's work over the semester. I let Gail ruin the celebration for me.

Crazy thoughts overwhelmed my thinking, even as I made polite conversation over lunch. *I am a Bible teacher. Can't I try something creative and fun occasionally? I bet I spent twenty hours working on that lesson and a lot more if you consider I had to learn how to apply stage makeup and look all over town for grey hair spray. She has no idea. And hey, I'm not paid a penny and I took more time away from David and the kids this week than usual. Does she appreciate the sacrifice? Noooo . . . I bet she has never taught anything. What does she know? I'm glad the semester is over and I hope she never comes back. I don't want to see her in the audience again—or anywhere else.*

A rather extreme reaction, don't you think, but honest. Gail was my first critic. Now thirty years later, as I reflect back, I'm embarrassed by my intense and immature reaction. In the next chapter, we will explore a variety of reasons *why* I and many women fail to react biblically and wisely when personally attacked or involved in a conflict. But first things first.

SURPRISE, SURPRISE

My mentors prepared me for my spiritual journey and ministry. They taught me to pray, study, and apply my Bible. They equipped me with a plethora of ministry skills—but *not one* ever mentioned to expect conflict. No one told me that *every* ministry leader, lay or paid, experiences criticism, personal attacks, and church politics. Don't believe me? Who would qualify as one of the most honest, amiable, godly Christian leaders alive today? I'm nominating the pastor of Stonebriar Community Church and Bible teacher on *Insight for Living*, Chuck Swindoll, who is also chancellor of the seminary where I teach. Now here is a man that no one would dare attempt to discredit, right? Surely he ministers so effectively that no one could find fault with his life and teaching. I thought so too until he stood at our chapel podium announcing, "There is not a week of my life that I don't receive hate mail. Not a week goes by that someone does not deliberately and personally criticize me inappropriately." [1]

Even Chuck Swindoll has critics like Gail. I just wish someone had told me about her. If I had only known to expect her, I would have prepared myself. I would not have been so vulnerable, so shocked, so wounded by her constructive criticism. And, by the way, it was constructive. She could have benefited from a shot of lovingkindness. She needed to learn healthy confrontational skills, but her point was valid. Now that I teach a seminary course *Women Teaching Women*, I hammer my students, nicely of course, with my conviction that even our dramatic presentations should be drawn from the text, without exception. Not that we deep-six creativity, but we must not substitute entertaining stories for God's truth. If I had been forewarned, I might have taken Gail's criticism to heart sooner and enjoyed my lunch. But like most unseasoned women, I was ignorant and ill-equipped to deal biblically and wisely with women who wound.

EVEN JESUS WAS NOT EXEMPT!

We learn from Jesus' earthly ministry, but here is one lesson often overlooked. Jesus lived with the Twelve for three years and among them was one who would betray Him. The Bible reveals that Jesus knew his heart.[2] Judas Iscariot had a secret agenda and Jesus was aware that Judas would sell Him out. Jesus felt the sting of conflict just like we do.

However Judas was not the only disciple to betray Jesus. Peter and the others scattered, scared to be associated with Jesus the day He was crucified. But Peter and the others returned to ask for forgiveness. Jesus was delighted to grant it and Jesus would have forgiven Judas too. But Judas would not return. He was his own worst enemy, choosing not to repent but to commit suicide instead. Judas is an example of a person who will not admit his fault and make peace. In the early stages of conflict, we don't know whether we are dealing with a Judas or a Peter. But we do know that if Jesus had His Judas, we can expect ours. But, take heart! In our experience, you will encounter many more women like Peter than like Judas.

PAUL WAS NOT EXEMPT EITHER

Paul endured a barrage of personal attacks and difficult people. After Jesus knocked him off his high horse on the Damascus Road, God put him through a preparation process that lasted fourteen years. During this time, the Jews put out a contract on him

and the Christians did not believe his conversion was real. He was
shuffled from Damascus to Jerusalem to Tarsus for protection
from assassins. Imagine the stinging verbal attacks and nasty behavior he encountered. It took Barnabas, a man the Christians
trusted, to convince believers that Paul was genuine.[3]

Even after his ministry was in high gear, he had run-ins with
Peter, the Judaizers,[4] and "some who preach Christ out of envy
and rivalry."[5] Paul writes that these charlatans "preach Christ out
of selfish ambition, not sincerely, supposing that they can stir up
trouble for me while I am in chains . . ."[6] Paul, like Jesus, occasionally faced harsh words, false accusations, and rude behavior.
Why are we so surprised when we find ourselves facing them too?

WOMEN'S LEADERS IN THE
BIBLE WERE NOT EXEMPT

Paul and the male leadership at Philippi mediated a "catfight"
between squabbling women. In his letter to the Philippian church
he writes, "I plead with Euodia and I plead with Syntyche to agree
with each other in the Lord. Yes, and I ask you, loyal yokefellow,
help these women who have contended at my side in the cause of
the gospel . . . "[7] Yes, women with great passion to serve Christ
clash. In a strange irony, the three women who have wounded me
most through my thirty-year ministry stint have been women
deeply committed to serving God. Later we will explore why.

GREAT WOMEN IN HISTORY WERE NOT EXEMPT

Even our larger-than-life heroines experienced conflict with
other women. For example, Abigail Adams, the wife of our second
president and mother of the sixth, stands as a tower of intellect,
faith, and fortitude,[8] a model to those who read her biographies
drawn from volumes of her letters preserved by historians. Yet
her letters reveal a heart-wrenching conflict she carried to her
grave. With husband John gone much of their married life, Abigail spent evenings corresponding with friends. One of the dearest was Mercy Warren, a woman of admirable intellect with whom
she interacted on questions regarding the revolution and the birth

of their beloved nation. For more than thirty years, these two astute women encouraged and inspired each other. As their friendship blossomed, Abigail wrote to Mercy, "Let your letters be of the journal kind. I could participate in your amusements, in your pleasures, and in your sentiments which would greatly gratify me, and I should collect the best of intelligence."[9] But in 1805, Mercy's three volumes on the American Revolution were published. Her work, according to both Abigail and John, contained numerous unflattering reports and "falsehoods" about John. "John, cut to the quick, took issue with Mercy passage by passage, all three volumes worth, initiating an exchange of ten long, involved letters of accusation and reproach that mounted to screaming pitch before they were done."[10]

Alas, Abigail and Mercy parted bitterly. When Mercy's husband died, Abigail wrestled with whether or not to at least send a note of sympathy:

> However, she recognized Mercy and John's fundamentally opposing political beliefs, and was sadly resigned to the fact that the bitterness of party spirit had severed them. After the injustice to John's character and the chance given Mercy to acknowledge her errors, which she wholly omitted to do, Abigail felt she had no alternative. "I thought a letter of the kind would appear insincere, and although I feel for her bereavement and know how heavily she must feel it, I have declined writing to her."[11]

Shortly before their deaths, tokens of forgiveness were offered and timidly accepted, but the fire of their friendship never rekindled.[12] How sad that these two women did not learn how to breach their differences, forgive one another, and restore their relationship—all possible through biblical peacemaking strategies.

WOMEN IN THE WORKPLACE ARE NOT EXEMPT

The American Management Association interviewed one thousand women in the marketplace to learn that 95 percent felt other women had undermined them some time during their careers.[13] Additional research revealed that woman-to-woman sabotage has increased by 50 percent in the last ten years.[14] Pat Heim and Susan Murphy, authors of *In the Company of Women*, conduct workshops all over the country on women's conflict in the workplace. When they ask the group, "When a woman gets promoted, who is the first to attack her?" the answer is always the same. "Women."[15]

EVEN HOLLYWOOD IS NOT EXEMPT

Superstar vocalist Barbra Streisand has sold eighty million records and earned millions of dollars from her recordings. She was honored with the Golden Globe's Cecil B. DeMille Award for her contribution to the entertainment industry. In a related article she said: "What I've done, going into a man's world was tough. You get attacked, but mostly by women. That's the irony. I've found that women are the most competitive and vitriolic. The worst reviews I've gotten were from women . . . When they're out to get you, they're out to get you.[16]

AND IT'S GETTING WORSE . . .

The ethos of ministry is affected by the culture, a surprise to some Christians. They expect that redeemed people will act like redeemed people. And many do, but some don't. The church attracts hurting people out of the culture who bring their woundedness, idiosyncrasies, and even their pathologies with them. Jesus heals them over time as they submit to Him. But in the meantime, some retain their meanness.

AS LONG AS THE FLESH IS WITH US . . .

Our flesh is that part of us that doesn't want to listen to God but instead wants to do its own thing. No matter how spiritually mature we become, we still battle our flesh. The flesh is with us until we die or Jesus comes back. Paul reveals the nature of our flesh in Galatians 5:17–21:

For the flesh has desires that are opposed to the Spirit . . .
these are in opposition to each other, so that you cannot do
what you want . . . now the works of the flesh are obvious:
sexual immorality, impurity, depravity, idolatry, sorcery, *hos-*
tilities, strife, jealousy, outbursts of anger, selfish rivalries,
dissentions, factions, envying, murder, drunkenness, carous-
ing, and similar things . . . (emphasis ours)

The bold italicized words describe emotions, attitudes, and
actions that create conflict. For example, our flesh is jealous when
others succeed. When a friend receives an honor we want, instead
of celebrating, our flesh says, "Why wasn't I chosen?" Pastor and
author John Maxwell followed in his preacher father's footsteps,
benefiting from his mentoring and leadership. As a result,
Maxwell experienced early success as the first in his denomination
to average more than a thousand in attendance every Sunday, the
youngest to write his first book, and the youngest to be elected to
a national office.

But a surprise accompanied his successes: "Unfortunately during those early years, I might have also been the loneliest pastor
in my denomination. The good news was that when I failed, plenty
of people were glad to commiserate with me. But when I succeeded, few celebrated. I thought my colleagues and I were on the
same team, but evidently they didn't see it that way. Many times
Margaret and I celebrated alone."[17]

Why didn't his colleagues celebrate with him? Probably because they struggled with jealousy, selfish rivalries, and envy that
can lead to dissentions and factions—straight out of Galatians
5:20.

The authors of the secular book *In the Company of Women* discuss this phenomenon. Of course, they don't call this phenomenon
"the flesh," a spiritual term. Instead they call it "The Power Dead-
Even Rule." They insist that when women in the workplace perceive themselves as dead even in their successes, all is well. But
when one of them is promoted and suddenly has more power or
prestige, the stage is set for a catfight: "In those situations in which

a woman's power is diminished (she loses her job, doesn't receive an expected promotion, or fails publicly), she finds her female co-workers to be extremely supportive. By contrast, when a woman has more power than another woman, behaves as if she has more power, or is perceived as trying to obtain more power, the environment is ripe for conflict."[18]

MIT graduate Dr. Leonard Sax agrees. In his book *Why Gender Matters*, he writes, "Girls' friendships work best when the friendship is between equals. If you're a girl or a woman and you think your friend believes herself to be 'better' than you, then your friendship with her is not likely to last. Boys on the other hand are comfortable in an unequal relationship, even if they are the lesser party."[19]

Maxwell, Heim, and Murphy suggest ways to overcome the Dead-Even Rule, and we will consider helpful methods and strategies throughout this book, but the point to remember now is that the flesh breeds conflict.

The flesh is real—even in Christians. We don't talk about these inner tensions because Christian women are supposed to be nice. Many of us deny we are ever jealous. When was the last time you heard anyone admit they struggle with this sin? But for so many women, at the moment our friend shines, our flesh winces. As we mature spiritually, we learn to overcome, to celebrate with others, and to shackle our dark side. But everyone is at a different place in the process—and emotionally immature and diseased women act out of their flesh. Expect it. To think otherwise is naïve. When you work with people in ministry, you have not entered the "no conflict zone."

Men kill their weak and women kill their strong.[20]

WHEN TODAY'S GIRLS BECOME WOMEN . . .

Conflict between females is different from conflict between males, as we will see in Chapter Two. Males generally display a more direct and sometimes more physical response to disputes. Most evenings, our local television news anchor paints the gory results of youth violence, and we expect the perpetrators to be boys. Usually they are. But according to the U.S. Department of Justice, "while criminal violence among teenage boys still far exceeds criminal violence among teenage girls, the gap is narrowing."[21] For every *ten* boys arrested for assault ten years ago, there was only one girl. Today there are only *four* boys arrested for every girl.[22]

James Garbarino says to expect a *new* American Girl:

> Girls in general are evidencing a new assertiveness and physicality that go far beyond criminal assault. They are apparent in the girls' participation in sports, their open sensuality, in their enjoyment of "normal" aggression that boys have long enjoyed in rough-and-tumble play, and in the feeling of confidence that comes with physical prowess and power. We should welcome the New American Girl's unfettered assertiveness and physicality. We should appreciate her athletic accomplishments, like the way she stands up for herself, and applaud her straightforward appreciation of herself as physical being. But I believe that the increasing violence among troubled girls are unintended consequences of the general increase in normal girls' getting physical and becoming more assertive.
>
> All this, the good news of liberation and the bad news of increased aggression, is the New American Girl.[23]

We predict that when the New American Girl grows up and joins the female ranks of the church, we can expect even more conflict, a good reason to arm ourselves now with biblical tools for the future.

WHY WE DON'T TALK ABOUT OUR CONFLICTS

We have seen that conflict is part of the human experience—no one is exempt, not Jesus, Paul, not people in the Bible or history. We can expect conflict and it's probably going to get worse. Then why don't we talk about it? Why do we fail to prepare for the inevitable? We believe one reason is because down deep we women feel that conflict is our own fault. When it comes to evaluating success and failure, men and women tend to think differently.

Girls on the average outperform boys in school (as measured by report card grades), in most subjects and in all age groups.[24] Because girls do better in school, one might imagine that girls would be more self-confident about their academic self-esteem. But that's not the case. Paradoxically, girls are more likely to be excessively critical in evaluating their own academic performance. Conversely, boys tend to have unrealistically high estimates of their own academic abilities and accomplishments.[25]

Women's beliefs about academic achievement spill over into other perceptions. For example, women tend to be harder on themselves, engage in negative self-talk, and advertise their flaws more than men. When females succeed, they tend to attribute their accomplishments to factors outside themselves—it was easy, I was lucky, I just worked hard. They seldom attribute their successes to their own abilities. But when females fail, they are quick to blame themselves. Interestingly, males have the opposite tendency. He is likely to attribute successes to his own abilities and failures to factors outside himself.[26]

This tendency to self-deprecation means that many women blame themselves for conflict. We are not saying women don't see their adversary as responsible too. But in the midst of the conflict, many women hear a condemning voice in their heads whispering, "I must be hard to get along with. I'm high maintenance, difficult, problematic. If I were just nicer, a better Christian, if I were more loving, if I worked harder, if … if … if …." an endless list of reasons why conflict points to personal failure. And so when conflict raises its ugly head, we are embarrassed and don't want anyone to know.

We especially don't want men to know. Talk about conflict, personal attacks, and church politics in a room full of women and you'll see nods of agreement and an eager desire to discuss the issue. But bring up the topic in mixed company and many women sit like stone. Why? Because "catfights" make women look bad. We don't want men to know women sometimes treat each other this way. We don't want to play into men's stereotypical thinking about women already. We experienced such thinking recently: when Kelley mentioned to her Sunday School class that she was beginning to work on a new book, this one about women in conflict, one of the men in her class deadpanned, "How many volumes?"

So, like ostriches, many of us suffer alone and in the dark, blaming ourselves and refusing to address the issue head-on or prepare for the next round. It's time to stop blaming ourselves. Yes, we may be part of the problem, but we are simply playing into Satan's traps when we refuse to acknowledge our shortcomings and work to acquire skills we will need later. Too many women jump ship, abandoning their callings when waters rise. Jesus needs you to take courage and learn to fight well.

Phyllis Chesler, author of *Woman's Inhumanity to Woman*, captures our intent in writing this book: "It is irresponsible to tell women that the world is safe when it is not. One must tell women to expect enemy fire down the road and deserters and collaborators within their own ranks. Such information will give women the option of adopting measures of self-defense."[27]

We want to give you the option of adopting measures that will enable you to stand tall in the midst of criticism, personal attacks, and church politics. But first, you must face facts. You won't be the exception and you are not odd, difficult, or bad when caught in conflict.

READY TO QUIT?

As you ponder these sobering stories, statistics, and research findings, do you wonder if serving Jesus is worth the hassle? To that question, we proclaim a resounding *yes!* Remember that only a small fraction of people you work with will be difficult. Most will support, appreciate, and encourage you. Unfortunately, we observe women allowing the 1 percent to overshadow the ninety-nine. The goal of this book is to equip you to deal positively with the one so you will not be sidelined from serving the ninety-nine. So keep on reading—solutions and strategies are ahead.

It is good for me that I have been afflicted, that I may learn Your statutes.

—**Psalm 119:71** NASB

Discussion *Questions*

1. Has anyone ever warned you to expect conflict and personal attacks in ministry? If so, specifically what did they say? If not, why do you think this is often a taboo topic?

2. In this chapter, we observed multiple biblical and historical examples of people enmeshed in disputes. Can you think of others?

3. Do you believe ministry conflicts and personal attacks are increasing? If so, why?

4. Have you observed more violence among girls and young women? Give examples.

5. What is the role of the "flesh" in conflict?

6. Have you personally experienced ministry conflict or personal attacks? How did you feel? (No names, please.)

7. Regardless of conflict in ministry, why is it rewarding to serve the Lord? How can you overcome the tendency to be discouraged by the few who are difficult?

Women's Ways *of* Whacking  Chapter 2

But avoid profane chatter, because those occupied with it
will stray further and further into ungodliness, and their
message will spread its infection like gangrene.

—2 Timothy 2:16–17

BREAKING RANK

In the introduction to her book *Woman's Inhumanity to Women*,
psychology professor Phyllis Chesler revealed that feminist leaders feared a book that talked about conflict among women, pre-
ferring to focus on "how men oppress women."[1] When Chesler, a
devoted champion of women's rights for more than forty years,
penned *The Death of Feminism* in 2005, "the sisterhood rewarded
her with excommunication."[2] We are grateful that Chesler had the
courage to break rank and research women's conflicts, and we join
her in the belief that we can no longer ignore the ways women
wound each other.

Next to my computer sits a stack of similar books by secular
authors with names like *Tripping the Prom Queen: The Truth About
Women and Rivalry* (Susan Barash); *Catfight: Rivalries Among
Women—From Diets to Dating, from the Boardroom to the Delivery
Room* (Leora Tanenbaum); *In the Company of Women: Indirect Ag-
gression Among Women, Why We Hurt Each Other and How to Stop*
(Pat Heim and Susan Murphy); *Odd Girl Out* (Rachel Simmons);
and *See Jane Hit* (James Garbarino).

All these books were released after 2000 and most are based

on research studies. Chesler loosed the floodgates, leading to a plethora of books on this hushed-up topic.

What can women in ministry learn from these books? None of them reflects a Christian perspective. Nevertheless, their research into the realities of women's conflicts helps us all understand ways the culture bleeds into ministry ethos today. Understanding these realities will ultimately help us work toward harmony, peace, and positive solutions.

Previously, we warned you to expect women who wound. Now we will explore specific ways women express their conflict with other women when they are acting out of their flesh, in the secular world and sometimes in the Christian world too. As women mature in Christ, we should see less and less of these types of behaviors. Remember our goal is to overcome these patterns so we can become skilled peacemakers, but before we can overcome them, we must recognize them. This chapter should help you spot difficult women.

To understand women's ways of conflict with more clarity, we will also contrast women's and men's conflict styles. This information will also help us when we tackle mixed-gender topics later in the book.

A DISCLAIMER

Whenever we talk about differences between men and women, "It is important for us to remember that averages reported about groups cannot give us reliable information about specific individuals."[3] Statements about the way women or men process conflict will not be true for everyone of that gender. If you don't fit the category, please don't berate yourself as lacking in femininity. Use these statistics, studies, and stories to help you formulate general patterns that are true in many cases, and as tools to help you work with both genders in conflict.

LITTLE GIRLS' GAMES

In the last chapter we observed that criminal violence among teenage girls is escalating. However, according to most research studies, girls and boys still exhibit different responses to conflict. For example, psychologist Janet Lever documented different ways girls and boys played on elementary school playgrounds during a one-year period. She discovered that girls seldom resorted to physical aggression when they disagreed. Instead, they fought with words—mean words. In contrast, boys fought physically, about twenty times more than girls. But these same boys usually ended up as better friends after the fight. They sought each other out as playmates, sometimes seeing the conflict as a bonding mechanism.

Boys played competitive games, but girls played games like jump rope and hopscotch, turn-taking games with lots of face time. These less competitive kinds of games never led to fist-fighting, but to more indirect aggression. And when girls entered into a conflict, they did not seek each other out the next day nor did they become good friends later. Bad feelings lasted and, in most cases, the girls were enemies for an extended period of time. In addition, she discovered that each girl was likely to foster a coalition of girls who took sides and followed suit.[4]

> For little girls, the game is never over. If they have a conflict, it is not readily forgiven and forgotten. In a study of preteens and teenagers at play, anthropologist Marjorie Harness Goodwin found that when girls strongly disapproved of one of their friend's behavior, they exercised the utmost social control by ostracizing her for up to six weeks.[5]

WOMEN'S INDIRECT STYLE

How does research on children's and teens' playgrounds translate into adult tendencies? Chesler writes:

> Recent studies and crime statistics confirm that men are aggressive in direct and dramatic ways. Although most women are not directly or physically violent, *women are highly aggressive, but in indirect ways.* The targets of such female aggression are not men—but other women and children. Researchers in

Europe, North America, and Australia have found that verbal and indirect aggression among girls and women include name-calling, insulting, teasing, threatening, shutting the other out, becoming friends with another as revenge, ignoring, gossiping, telling bad stories behind a person's back, and trying to get others to dislike that person.6 (emphasis ours)

Heim and Murphy agree. They define women's indirect aggression as "covert aggression: we are mounting an attack in such a way that we hope to remain hidden, and we do this to protect ourselves: we disguise our hostile intentions in order to avoid retaliation and social condemnation."[7] They list gossip, spreading rumors and divulging secrets, publicly making insinuations and insulting comments, undermining and sabotaging, and purposefully snubbing and withdrawing friendship as common characteristics of indirect aggression.[8]

WOMEN'S FEAR OF OPEN CONFLICT

Why do women choose indirect means when they fight? Why is it so difficult for many women to speak openly and honestly about their disagreements? Consider the results of current research. These findings are not true for all women but they do seem to represent many women. We can learn female tendencies, as well as male, that will help us learn to manage conflict positively.

First, every study on gender differences in the last thirty years concludes that women value connections, living in a "web of relationships," while men value autonomy and a "hierarchy of power."[9] Women see life through a relational lens, even making decisions on the basis of how that decision will affect people they love. Women often evaluate their identity and security in terms of their relationships. Consequently many women feel safest in the center of a web of relationships while many men feel safest at the top of the hierarchy.[10]

As a result, to many women, conflict is a threat to connectedness, to be avoided at all costs. However, conflict is a fact of life.

We can't avoid it—but instead of openly discussing the disagreement, women tend to go underground with their conflict. Disputes are preferably settled without direct confrontation, in direct disobedience to Scripture, a phenomenon that we will explore later.

Second, we must consider the way little girls are raised, or socialization. From the day our families take us home from the hospital, they model and teach us how to live as either a boy or a girl. Our schools, church, and community also play a major role in shaping us, according to an acceptable standard of attitudes and actions. Of course, this shaping varies from family to family and country to country, but in most contexts, boys and girls are raised differently.

Reports of such gender-related differences are legion in social psychology journals. Research has shown that fathers frequently carry their baby boys in one arm (the way a running back might tuck a football into the crook of his arm), while they often hold baby girls more carefully with both hands, caress them closer to the chest, and cuddle them more than boys. Boys are tossed into the air and roughhoused; they are tickled more. We allow them to cry longer before we pick them up, while we often attend to girls as soon as they make the first peep. This may teach girls at a very young age that someone will pay attention, soothe their pain, and try to meet their needs—whereas boys are taught to tough it out.[11]

Again these generalities are not true for every female, but by and large, girls are socialized to be soft, sweet, and nice. Combine niceness with girls' relational bent and you have a formula for indirect aggression. Conflict interferes with friendship and niceness; it means we disagree about something. The harmony of the relationship is threatened. So, many females gravitate toward indirect means of showing their grievances.

I (Sue) have often observed this tendency in women. For example, during the past thirty years, I have led and participated in literally hundreds of small groups of women, usually related to Bible studies that foster deep discussions about life and God. Few women in those groups know how to disagree agreeably. When a diverse opinion surfaced, most of the women squirmed. If the "heated" discussions became the norm, women dropped out of the group, but they almost never articulated their discomfort *in* the group. They fabricated reasons for leaving or came to me, the leader, to complain. For years, I participated in their pathologies by listening to their protests and accusations, believing I was helping them "work through" their feelings. However, now I refuse to listen, insisting that they take their complaints to the person who "offended" them, a biblical response, as we will see later.

MEN'S DIRECT STYLE

Why do men exhibit a more direct conflict style? Again, sociologist Janet Lever's research with children on elementary playgrounds is helpful. Boys played their competitive games in large groups, allowing any boy with the "right stuff" regardless of age to join in. Girls played their less competitive games in smaller, more homogeneous groups. She argues that play prepares boys and girls with needed social and vocational skills later in life.

Boys' games provide a valuable learning environment. It is reasonable to expect that the following social skills will be cultivated on the playground: the ability to deal with diversity in memberships where each person is performing a special task; the ability to coordinate actions and maintain cohesiveness among group members; the ability to cope with a set of impersonal rules; and the ability to work for collective as well as personal goals. Team sports furnish the most frequent opportunity to sharpen these social skills. One could elaborate on the lessons learned. The rule structure encourages strategic thinking. Team sports also imply experience with clearcut leadership positions, usually based on universalistic criteria. The group rewards the individual who has improved valued skills, a practice which further enhances a sense of confidence, based on achievement. *Furthermore, through team sports as well as individual matches, boys learn to deal with interpersonal competition in a forthright manner. Boys experience face-to-face confrontation—often opposing a close friend—and must learn to depersonalize the attack.* They must practice self-control and sportsmanship; in fact, some of the boys in this study described the greatest lesson in team sports as learning to "keep your cool."[12] (emphasis ours)

Lever argues that boys learn direct ways to disagree on the playground. They carry these skills into adulthood, resulting in more overt methods when they face conflict. Of course, again, this is not true for all men, but it is for the majority. The question is: now that girls are more involved in competitive sports, will they be more direct as adults? Time will tell.

LESSONS FROM THE CLASSROOM

Whether you believe that boys are naturally drawn to competitive play or that the games make the man, the effect of years of competition may explain the differences I observe in my seminary classroom. I encourage frank discussion in my courses, a powerful tool that draws students into the material and encodes it in the minds of many kinds of learners. My first semester as a seminary professor, a few male students challenged other male students, even occasionally using combative language in interchanges with me. Initially, I took their confrontation as a sign of disrespect, but I did not become defensive or unkind in my responses, a strong temptation at times. I entered into their questions without taking personal offense, and often a provocative interaction resulted. The next semester, I did create discussion ground rules, one of the first-day-of-class handouts. I insisted that they disagree and phrase their comments "respectfully."

I'm glad I did, because these guidelines set a tone that welcomes the participation of the women students. But I also noticed something I had not expected. The male students who challenged me and other students, "respectfully" or otherwise, were the male students who often sought out a friendship with me as the semester progressed. They gave the course high marks on their evaluations and seemed to respect me more for allowing this kind of interaction. And our friendships continue, as I fill out reference forms for employment after graduation and send baby gifts as they start their families. This provocative interchange and bantering opened a door and seemed to cement lasting friendships with my male students, a phenomenon I never experienced with women.

One semester I was team-teaching a course on small group dynamics with a male colleague. We trained students to lead small groups and gave them each an opportunity to try out their skills by leading a Bible study lesson in class. One bright, edgy male led the mixed-gender group into a firestorm of controversy that resulted in the men arguing and interrupting each other to drive home their points. I watched the women carefully. They sat wide-eyed and wary. Afterward, in the evaluation, the women confessed their discomfort and fear that this "unkind" exchange would shatter relationships in the group. The men, including my male colleague, were dumbfounded.

DIFFERENT LENSES

During the last ten years, I have participated in a variety of weekly gatherings (church staff, seminary department, and faculty meetings) all male-led and far outnumbering women in attendance. Occasionally the men would raise their voices, pound the table, and exchange heated words in a debate-like style. I have yet to enter one of these exchanges, nor have any of my female colleagues. When the ethos heats up, we women clam up.

How can men disagree so strongly and not be wounded the way women almost always are? If Lever is correct, men learn as boys to compete *impersonally* and to compartmentalize the conflict. Barash agrees,

Guys compete, sure, but their contests tend to be *specific, goal-oriented, and limited*. They may fight to the death over who

scores the most points . . . who snags a much-desired promotion, or drives the bigger car, but these contests are generally
limited to one specific area of competition, and *when it's over, it's
truly over* . . . While men are cutting each other out of deals and
potential clients, they're usually not also looking at who's
gained weight, whose kids are failing geometry, or who's having a bad hair day. Women's competition, by contrast, *extends
simultaneously into all realms* . . . Women's competition, by contrast, is about our identities—and unlike men, we tend to expect total union and sympathy with our same-sex friends. We
have a much harder time setting boundaries to our competition, which makes it all the more destructive.[13] (emphasis ours)

Men and women seem to view conflict through different
lenses—men see conflict as the way to compete in the world, and
sometimes, as I have shown, even as a means to establish connections. It's not personal. It's expected. It's the way brothers compete, jockeying for the top of the heap. Men argue for their
position with red faces, but afterward, go out for lunch and forget
it. The interchange was specific and limited to that situation, and
now it's over.

But for women it's personal, and many times, it's never over—
not unless they commit to the hard work of working through
emotions and deep woundedness, our goal in this book. For some
women, if you raise your voice and contradict me, you must dislike *me*. I am cut to the core. You are no longer my friend, no
longer on my team. Your rejection extends to the depths of who
I am. You have threatened the very thing that gives me security
and safety—my relationship with you and probably with others,
since you are likely to extend this conflict beyond yourself. As a
result, many women see direct conflict as a threat to relationships,
to be avoided at all costs. So women employ indirect means—all
that stuff that labels women as catty, malicious, and manipulative.

No wonder we observe damaging conflict among women in
ministry. But don't be discouraged. Jesus knows these tendencies

and has given us clear instructions on how to overcome them. We are not prisoners to natural gender habits as we will see later.

WOMEN'S SPECIFIC UNDERGROUND TACTICS

We have seen that women and men approach conflict differently. Let's look more closely at some of the indirect tactics employed by women acting out of their flesh.

On the first day of a new job, Lana's new colleagues were so friendly that she opened up, sharing that she was taking night-school classes and was on a new diet. However, the second day when all the women were in a meeting with the boss, some questions came up about office procedure. One of the "friendly" women said, "Why don't we ask Lana how to settle this? When she gets her wonderful new degree, she'll be off to a better job, so we should take advantage of her while she is here!" The boss, who did not know about these plans, gave Lana a funny look. And Lana wondered if her new friend was really a friend after all.

Later another of Lana's new "friends" stopped by her desk with a plate of goodies. "I know you're dieting," she said sweetly, "but I just had to bring you one of my homemade muffins. Don't you just love chocolate?" When Lana tried to refuse, the baker looked hurt—or was it angry—and Lana wondered if maybe she'd been too friendly.

We have all been there. A woman offers a suggestion that indirectly implies criticism. My mother has been seriously ill for many years, requiring us to cancel our vacations several times. A female friend remarked that surely her surgeries could be rescheduled, implying that we let my mother take advantage of us. These covert comments were so nicely packaged in caring conversation that I wondered at first why I felt resentful. Then I deciphered the indirect criticism and was irritated. But who am I to throw stones? I am guilty too. I'm sure my daughters could give examples of when I have buried my criticism this way, but my intense motherly love is no excuse for pigs-in-a-blanket criticism because "Mother knows best." I work hard to eliminate these kinds of tactics because I know they hurt our relationship.

Here is another example of typical indirect female tactics. A woman gives you a compliment that contains hidden criticism. "I loved your lecture. Finally I was able to follow your thinking." Hmmm, she was praising your efforts but at the same time informing you that generally your thinking is muddy. Or how about "I love your new apartment. The colors work so much better than your last one." Thanks a lot.

Another way to appear kind while actually hurting another is to repeat a critical comment made by someone else. "Jennifer told me that the quality of the Bible study is terrible this year. I just thought you should know." And of course, there is the infamous sharing of prayer requests—spiritualizing those tasty morsels of gossip in a pretense of care.

Women also exhibit this underground aggression when they speculate about another woman's motives or flaws. For example, during an intense year of ministry when I was near burnout, a woman on the leadership team began to ask the other women to pray for me because I "had lost focus" and she was afraid I "did not care about the women anymore." I remember another incident when a program we launched did not seem to be working as well as we had expected. One of my leaders began to ask the other women if perhaps I might not be praying as fervently as I should, thereby causing the problem, and of course, asking them all to pray for me. Buried seeds of dissension. These women were comrades but later turned out to be instigators of serious conflict. They began with indirect aggression couched in sugary care, concern, and niceness.

SAD STATISTICS IN THE SECULAR WORLD

How prevalent is woman-to-woman conflict in the secular world? In a study of five hundred women, from a variety of ethnic groups, ages, and faiths, the results were:

- first, that women in the secular business world were still willing to cut one another's throats over what they valued most—jobs, men, and social approval.

- second, that women will do anything rather than face up
  to female envy and rivalry. "Between traditional social
  pressures to be the 'good girl' and feminist expectations
  of solidarity, we sweep all evidence of a bleaker picture
  under the rug."[14]

From women working in the highest levels of socio-
economic status to the lowest, testimonies from the secular professional and business world echo a sad refrain.

Maybe it's because being a surgeon is so macho that the
women surgeons I know treat each other so horribly . . . Each
year another woman appears on the scene and at first I think,
"Wow, this is great, the more women, the better off we all will
be." But that isn't the case. What happens is that we act like
we care about one another and we all meet for drinks, once a
month, to talk about how tough the male discrimination is.
But it's a sham . . . At the last meeting, one of the women was
complaining about a male surgeon in her division. She said
that he wasn't really capable and that a woman with such low
standards would never have a job at this hospital. One of the
other women doctors actually reported her remarks to the department. The doctor was chastised and asked to apologize,
and it became an ordeal. I wasn't surprised. I knew that my female peers were there more to get information about other
doctors than they were to help one another succeed.[15]

Compare the doctor's story with that of a female bus driver.

This is the same as any other job, you have your friends, and
there are people who are not your friends. And those women
are against you. There aren't many women bus drivers, so
you'd think we'd stick together, but we don't. When I first
came on this job, I thought, wow, there are only a handful of
women and mostly we are of the same race, and this could
work out. We understand each other, I thought. But just be-

cause we understand each other doesn't mean we're there for each other . . . Sometimes I feel closer to some of the women passengers who I'm driving than to my female coworkers.[16]

SHOULDN'T IT BE DIFFERENT IN THE CHURCH?

Yes, it should be different in the church, and it is. I (Sue) have enjoyed wonderful relationships with women in the church and the academy. In my early years as a Christian, spiritual mothers and mentors guided me. They taught me how to love God, my husband, and children as well as to teach the Bible, lead small groups, and write curriculum. When I began to lead women's ministries in the church, women joined me. We envisioned what God could do and we watched Him implement our dreams. These women cheered me on when I succeeded and when I messed up. One of my greatest delights has been to have a part in launching them as they pursue their dreams for God.

It was a woman who walked with me as I attempted to write my first book. Today, I write with women because I love the camaraderie and insight they bring to each project. And God provided a great female friend in the academy. We work and team-teach in the same department. We are different in temperament and gift-mix, but complement and support each other in a world dominated by men.

Women have been a source of tremendous joy, but like every other woman I know in ministry, a few women have also wounded me deeply. These women have been my cohorts, my dearest friends—yet, in time, several turned on me and attempted to destroy my reputation and ministry. Elizabeth Holland, a nineteenth-century writer, said, "As nobody can do more mischief to a woman than a woman, so perhaps one might reverse the maxim and say nobody can do more good."[17] I have experienced both.

IT ONLY TAKES ONE . . .

Fortunately, my adversaries have been few. In thirty years, only three women have betrayed me, wounding me deeply. Despite multiple yet imperfect efforts these women would not make peace. Two partnered together in a single incident that lasted more than a year. The other emerged when the ministry was struggling and attempted a coup. She wanted my job and went to great lengths to get it. These three women made some days of ministry miserable for two of my thirty years of ministry. During those years, I considered quitting. I'm so glad I didn't.

And if a certain former friend and partner in ministry were writing this book, she would undoubtedly name me as the woman who wounded her. If I could have a "do over" in life, this would be it. Although there were lessons for both of us, none of us is innocent, because we are all sinners, flawed and in process. Thankfully, major conflict is rare, though devastating at times, especially for women.

In addition, every year there will be skirmishes. Dealing with them is part of being a leader. There were always the women who did not like something I taught or said or did. I recall a few who were unhappy with their small group, or because I forced them to create new groups each year, or because I insisted that the retreat budget be part of the women's ministry budget. But after sitting down to talk, we worked out the grievance, often based on a misunderstanding or a difference in philosophy. These meetings were always hypercharged emotionally because, like most women, I don't like confrontation. But I have learned its value. It's not an option—because it only takes one out-of-control conflict to make ministry miserable. It only takes one to sabotage all your hard work.

The good news is that all of us can learn to face these difficult women and, in most cases, overcome our disagreements and make peace. If I had been better prepared, I might have worked out more positive solutions with the three women who hurt me so deeply. I was oversensitive and ignorant. Our prayer is that you won't make the same mistakes.

THE POINT

Why have we spent a whole chapter on secular research about gender tendencies? Because we want you to see that conflict is the norm. Don't go looking for it, but don't be shocked when it happens. It is rampant in the secular world and it can bleed into ministry. Expect it. We also want you to understand that women tend toward indirect aggression so you can spot this in others and work to eliminate it in yourself.

But first, the challenge is for us to know ourselves—to acknowledge our own feelings and flaws. Only then can we become skilled peacemakers, catalysts to positive outcomes. The next chapter will help.

Pursue peace with everyone, and holiness, for without it no one will see the Lord. See to it that no one comes short of the grace of God, that no one be like a bitter root springing up and causing trouble, and through him many become defiled.

—Hebrews 12:14–16

Discussion*Questions*

1. What differences have you observed in ways boys and girls play and communicate?

2. Do you believe gender differences are designed by God, the result of socialization, or both? Discuss graciously.

3. What differences have you observed in ways adult men and women approach and process conflict?

4. Have you experienced women's indirect style in conflict? Can you give specific examples?

5. How might these differences affect a mixed-gender ministry team?

6. Does conflict quickly escalate to a personal level for you or are you able to compartmentalize the issue? How do these tendencies affect your feelings and behavior in conflict?

Prepare Personally *for* Women Who Wound

Chapter 3

Finally, brothers and sisters, rejoice, set things right, be
encouraged, agree with one another, live in peace,
and the God of love and peace will be with you.

—2 Corinthians 13:11–12

Eva Mozes Kor and her twin sister were guinea pigs in the horrific Auschwitz experiments of Holocaust doctor Josef Mengele.
Eva lived through the ordeal but her sister died of complications.
Eva's decision to forgive the doctor shocked the world and drew
harsh criticism from other Holocaust survivors. Eva insisted that
forgiving her oppressors enabled her to heal and move on with
her life. When a young Jewish girl asked for counsel, Eva answered, "To live in this ——— ——— world, you have to be tough."[1]

Women in lay or vocational ministry are unlikely to face this
sort of harsh abuse. However, Eva Kor's advice is still fitting—
to serve God in ministry, you have to be tough. As Stuart Briscoe
said, "Qualifications of a pastor: the mind of a scholar, the heart of
a child and the hide of a rhinoceros."[2]

In thirty years of counseling women, I (Sue) have observed
that most women in ministry lack the required thick skin. They
are people-pleasers. A few bulldoze their way through conflict,
blind to the damage they leave in their wake. But others are more
likely to be addicted to approval. Both people-pleasers and bulldozers are particularly vulnerable in conflict.

GRACE AND ANGELA

Attorney Grace owned a twenty-six-year-old law practice focused on helping women through tough divorces and abuse. The practice flourished despite her ongoing battle with several benign brain tumors, requiring multiple surgeries that resulted in slight ocular damage. She hired Angela as one of her paralegals, but after six years, her associates reported that Angela was slacking off on the job. Grace scheduled several face-to-face meetings with Angela, explaining her expectations and giving Angela opportunity to improve. Angela quit.

The next week, Grace began receiving emails from Angela full of crazy accusations. She demanded vacation pay she was not entitled to. She alleged harassment. She threatened to sue. Grace invited Angela to sit down and talk about their differences. Her tone was kind but firm, but Angela refused. For several weeks, her complaints and ranting continued, grieving the whole staff. Then they abruptly stopped.

A year later, Grace saw Angela's name come across her email. Grace drew in a deep breath as she opened the message that read: *I guess we are not so different after all. I have just been to the doctor and I have a brain tumor. Please pray for me.*

Grace wrote back: *I'm so sorry. Are you in the hospital? Can I see you? We will pray. What can I do?* Angela responded with the details. When she was wheeled into her hospital room from surgery, Grace was there. She brought her ice cream, brushed her hair, and helped her recover. They never spoke about the earlier accusations or unkind emails.

Two weeks after Angela was released from the hospital, she showed up at Grace's law practice. Amidst whispers from her staff, Grace invited Angela into her office. Within an hour, Angela prayed to accept Christ, hugged Grace, and asked for forgiveness.

This story is true, although details have been altered to protect the identities of Grace and Angela. Grace is my (Sue's) student, a seasoned Christian, who lives what she proclaims. Angela was foolish to threaten to sue an attorney. But Grace did not use her advantages to win over Angela. Grace loved her enemy and

God used her love to woo Angela to Jesus.

Grace is neither a people-pleaser nor a bulldozer. She models the actions and attitudes that make peace far more likely—a goal for us all to emulate. Grace walks intimately with Christ and Grace knows herself.

KNOW YOURSELF

To be successful as a peacemaker, your top priority is to pursue emotional health. Work hard on the inner you. We all have baggage, problems, hurts, weaknesses, faults, quirks, idiosyncrasies, and sin. We hurt because we were not loved perfectly by our parents, spouses, or friends. We lack a mother who cheered us on or a father who protected us. We have no extended family or a quirky extended family. We all share this human condition— we all live in a fallen world.

The question is what have we done with our lack? Have we used it to excuse immaturity? Or have we committed to the hard work of achieving emotional health? Only emotionally healthy women respond wisely when personally attacked or entangled in conflict.

IDENTITY ISSUES

In conflicts, we sometimes endure verbal jabs. Our opponent labels us as too sensitive, bossy, busy, or driven. We are incompetent. We don't pray, care, or delegate enough. She charges that the conflict was caused by something we did or failed to do. These accusations can cause us to question ourselves, even when we know our identity is based in Christ.

The Identity Conversation looks inward; it's all about who we are and how we see ourselves. How does what happened affect my self-esteem, my self-image, my sense of who I am in the world? What impact will it have on my future? What self-doubts do I harbor? In short: before, during, and after the difficult conversation, the Identity Conversation is about what I am saying to myself about me.[3]

Stone, Patton, and Heen of the Harvard Negotiation Project list three core identity issues that concern most of us when we find ourselves in the midst of conflict: Am I competent? Am I a good person? Am I worthy of love? If our identity is threatened, we will probably react poorly in the conflict.[4]

They also suggest that we are most vulnerable when we fall prey to extreme "all-or-nothing" thinking; either we are completely competent or hopelessly incompetent, thoroughly good or horribly bad, and worth loving or worthless.[5] To fight these tendencies, give yourself grace. We all make mistakes and have much to learn. An emotionally healthy woman grounds her identity in Jesus and works to understand when identity issues are making her overly sensitive, abrasive, or foolish.

For specifics on effective conversation strategies, read Difficult Conversations: How to Discuss What Matters Most *by Douglas Stone, Bruce Patton, Sheila Heen, and Roger Fisher. Although the spiritual dimension is missing, they have written a practical handbook on what to say during the conflict resolution process, and how to say it well. We highly recommend this book for both men and women.*

In addition to a healthy self-image based in Christ, an emotionally healthy woman like Grace must guard against pride, a sin leading to qualities that render her particularly vulnerable in conflict.

THE SUBTLE SIN OF PRIDE

Angela exhibited a proud, arrogant attitude. How would you identify someone who is proud? How do proud people act? Proud people boast and name drop. They feel superior because of what they drive, where they live, and what they wear. Proud people are narcissistic and selfish. They think the whole world revolves around them. It is easy to recognize these people as proud. Most

Christian women, particularly leaders, don't identify with this kind of pride.

But pride is also a subtle heart attitude that sneaks up and grabs us before we know it. This kind of pride masquerades as personal ambition. And this is the kind of pride Christian leaders battle. This kind of pride takes various forms: insisting on our own way, believing we are indispensable to God's work, and thinking different is wrong. Pride is bashing someone's reputation, even subtly, and enjoying it. Pride is thinking we alone know how to fix others. Pride loves the spotlight. Proud people see other people's faults clearly but expect others to understand that they "just had a bad day." Proud people expect grace but seldom extend it.

Pride is who we are when we don't depend on God. It is the mature Christian's Achilles' heel. It is the natural state of our flesh and most of us disguise it effectively. Often it is only those who live with us who know we have a pride problem. And we *all* do if we are not intentional about combating our natural tendency toward pride. This is why the Bible warns us over and over to identify and eradicate the subtle sin of pride.

Sneaky, sneaky pride. When God blesses you or opens a door and you think you did it yourself, you are proud. If you are judgmental, you are proud. If it's your way or the highway, you are proud. If you minister for the accolades of others, you are proud. If you think you are humble, you are proud. Pride is often at the root of badly resolved conflict. Timothy Dwight, president of Yale College in the late 1700s, describes pride this way:

> No passion of the human mind is stronger than this. After it has been sufficiently indulged, it becomes so habitual that it occupies all the energy of the soul—or perhaps more accurately, it becomes all the energy of the soul, transforming all of the soul's faculties and all its efforts into servants of its own selfish purposes. In such cases, the soul is changed into a mere mass of ambition; and nothing in heaven, or in earth, is valued except to the extent that it can serve his master ambition . . . There is no excess, no length to which this passion will not

go. There is no authority of God or man against which it will
not rebel; no law which it will not violate; no obligation which
it will not neglect; no pure motive which it will not overcome.
There is no other form of wickedness that can become more
intense, nor its plan more vast, nor its obstinancy more enduring, nor its destruction more extensive, or more dreadful
than the love of distinction.[6]

Again, our first order of business if we want to serve Jesus
well is to be ruthless in our pursuit of emotional health. Pay the
price, carve out the time, do whatever is necessary to be healthy
from the inside out. Two unhealthy qualities that stem from pride
can hinder a woman's effectiveness in resolving conflict: people-
pleasing and bulldozing.

Defining people-pleasing

The Disease to Please is a set of self-defeating thoughts and
flawed beliefs about yourself and other people that fuel compulsive behavior that, in turn, is driven by the need to avoid forbid-
den, negative feelings. This triple combination of distorted
thinking, compulsive behavior, and the need to avoid fearful
feelings creates the syndrome of people-pleasing . . .

—Harriet Braiker[7]

People-pleasers are enslaved to flawed beliefs, feelings, and
behaviors that make them easy targets for unhealthy adversaries
and ineffective as peacemakers. People-pleasers are approval addicts. They want everyone to be happy—peace at any price.

Is it wrong to want to please people? No, the Bible instructs
us to care about the needs of others, to be considerate and kind.
When we treat people well, they usually treat us well too—the
Golden Rule. Societies function well when people are civil, honest,

even heroic as they interact with others. But pleasing people has a negative side too. Lou Priolo writes, "It is right to please people to the extent that doing so is not the leading principle or primary motive of your actions, but subordinate to the love of God and the love of neighbor."[8] However, we don't always know our motivation—why we do what we do. It's easy to believe that our primary interest is glorifying God when really a higher goal is our own self-interest, being liked and feeling good about ourselves.

Priolo labels people-pleasing as *idolatry*, a two-sided coin: one side involves neglecting God and the other side involves replacing Him with a cheap substitute, in this case people. When we desire the accolades of people more than God or we fear the rejection of people more than the displeasure of God, then we are people-pleasers.[9] If our parents and teachers taught us that the way to please God is to be compliant and nice, which is true for many Christian women, it's easy to become muddled as to our motivation. Many Christian women unconsciously fall prey to people-pleasing, an insidious form of pride.

Dr. Hans Selye, the father of modern concepts of stress and stress-induced illness, has another name for people-pleasing. He calls it "altruistic egoism."[10]

This mouthful of a phrase is intended to mean that by earning the goodness of others through the generosity of your character and actions, you are actually acting in your own self-interest. If you are kind and giving to others, Selye argued, other people will tend to be kind in return and, therefore, won't be as likely to cause you stress . . . Dr. Selye understood that niceness would not protect you from everyone, all of the time. He was adamant that certain people could and would cause harm to you emotionally—regardless of whether you treated them kindly or not. This might occur because the other person is intrinsically hateful, prejudiced or bigoted; or because he or she holds an old grudge and is out to settle a score by punishing you; or simply because the other person is not emotionally healthy or mature enough to be loved and to love in return.[11]

CHARACTERISTICS AND COST
What traits typify people-pleasers?

1. Perfectionism

If we are perfect and if our work is perfect, then everyone will love us and no one will criticize us, right? The problem is that we are finite humans in process. Until we accept that truth about ourselves and others, and give up perfectionism, we cannot thrive in ministry. If we are perfectionists, we analyze our work under a microscope for errors instead of gazing through a telescope for the big picture. Leaders work *on* the ministry, not *in* the ministry, tweaking strategies to keep the ministry moving forward.

It's admirable to strive for excellence, but foolish to expect perfection. Excellence pursues high standards, but leaves room for mistakes and even expects them.

The cost of perfectionism is that we are robbed of the satisfaction of a job well done. And we judge ourselves and everyone around us with an impossible standard that breeds discontent and dissatisfaction. Perfectionists resist delegating and waste time focusing on details, missing the main things—death to effective leadership.

2. Inability to say "no"

People-pleasers are like toy soldiers with windup handles sticking out of their backs. People wind you up and set you down to march to their beat, unaware that others are also directing your energies and steps. If you can't keep people off your back, because your highest priority is pleasing them, then your life is a maze of misdirected steps. Effective leaders manage their time and energy carefully, and they do not allow other people to oversee their calendars. Say "no" and, remember, you don't owe anyone an explanation.

Christian women are notorious for overcommitting, for feeling like they never do enough, and for endless striving. Again, we are taught to serve, and serving is good unless we serve to be accepted and appreciated by people. If that is our motivation we have stepped over the line into people-pleasing. If we do, we are easily manipulated, abused, and stressed.

My near burnout occurred slowly—like the frog in the pot. I'm told if you put a frog in a pot of cold water, he won't jump out. If you gradually increase the heat, he adjusts—until you can boil him to death and he doesn't even know. I accepted two "part-time" positions—one at seminary and one in the local church. At first, the load was doable. I loved my work, but over the years, as each ministry grew, the weight bore down. And when I added writing a book and earning another degree to the load, I almost went under. Stress creeps up until you find yourself backed into a corner of commitment. In that corner, you are especially vulnerable if conflict erupts. I learned the hard way to say "no."

And stress takes a physical toll. Duke Robinson tells this story.

One evening at our home in Oakland, in the early seventies, I stepped outside to whistle for Raider, our little black and silver terrier. But when I pursed my lips, nothing happened. I tried several times but to no avail, and I noticed that my chin and lips felt numb. I'd always been a great whistler, so my surprise quickly turned to concern. A few days later in my doctor's office, I took a dozen tests and answered a hundred questions, with no sign of physical problems. Finally, he turned to me and asked, "How many hours per week do you work on average?" I told him I did not know but it was probably too many. He asked me to take the next three weeks to chart those hours and scheduled me for another appointment. As we sat down in his office for that second visit, I handed him a slip of paper that said *68 hours per week*. He said, "Your inability to whistle is an early warning sign that you're not running your life correctly."[12]

Duke scaled back his workweek and the whistle soon came back. Stress is a dangerous ingredient in conflict and can hurt or kill us physically. Monitor your stress.

If perfectionism is about the quality of our work, the inability to say "no" is about the quantity of our work. Both scream, "If I am good enough, you will approve of me. You won't criticize, abandon, or reject me." Dream on, sister.

3. Dishonesty
   People-pleasers are dishonest, not morally, but socially. If you care too much about pleasing people, you won't honestly tell them what you think. You can't help people on self-destructive paths because you are too concerned that they might reject you. In a world crying for authenticity, you are shackled. Honesty is a prerequisite quality for skilled peacemaking.

My **biggest flaw** is my inability to confront people. After all the shows I've done, the books I've read, the psychologists I've talked to, I still allow myself to get ripped off to the nth degree. It takes days and days of procrastinating and agonizing before I can work up the nerve to say anything. Sometimes I think I'd rather just run out and get hit by a truck than confront someone who is ripping me off, hoping I would take up their cause.

—**Oprah Winfrey**[13]

4. Defensiveness and oversensitivity
   Someone once said that criticism did not bother him unless it was from a stranger, an acquaintance, a coworker, a friend, or a family member.[14] I can relate. My natural tendency is to be a people-pleaser, for years resulting in oversensitive defensiveness when I was criticized.

   She is oversensitive to correction, reproof, and other allusions of dissatisfaction or disapproval on the part of others. The people-pleaser overreacts to any hint of disapproval. She feels a pinprick as keenly as a knife in the back. She is overly sensitive because she is too concerned about her own glory (and popularity). She sees any constructive criticism or suggestion for improvement as a threat to her reputation rather than an opportunity to grow as an indication of the reprover's love for her.[15] (pronouns changed from masculine to feminine)

My people-pleasing resulted from growing up performing for approval and love, and, of course, because I am a sinner. Fortunately I married a man who loves me unconditionally. He helped me trust Jesus, accept myself, and leave people-pleasing behind. He did not overreact when someone criticized him—a great model for me to emulate. We observed in Chapter Two that many men are able to limit criticism to specifics. In other words, if a banquet guest complains about cold pork chops, my husband was able to limit criticism to the cold pork chops, allowing him to focus on a solution for the future.

I, on the other hand, would have taken the comment about the cold pork chops personally. *Oh, no, this means I did not choose a good caterer for the banquet. I've never been any good with pork. I am not even a good cook. My mother said I would never be any good as a pork chop chef, and it's true. And if the main course was a failure, then the whole meal was probably cold too. Oh, no, the banquet is ruined and I'm probably going to lose my position as banquet chair. Next year they will expel me from the women's ministry team. What will my friends think? I may never have the opportunity to serve women again. I'm going to grow old alone, a recluse. I never want to look a pork chop in the face again. And this is probably going to destroy the women's ministry anyway. It's our biggest event. Like dominoes, the whole ministry is going down, and it's all my fault.* This train of thought has snaked its way through the people-pleaser's mind by the time the complainer has finished her cold pork chops complaint.

The food critic now stares into the teary eyes of a devastated, barely functioning woman whose hurt is about to turn to anger at the injustice of it all. The complainer had no idea that the future of the women's ministry rested on the back of a cold pork chop. Constructive results are unlikely when one party thinks like this. People-pleasers must control their thoughts and emotions, allowing for productive solutions. Oversensitive defensive women sabotage the peacemaking process before it begins.

5. Easily manipulated and exploited

When strong women get wind that you are a people-pleaser, watch out. They seem to sense when you are vulnerable. If you seem overly sensitive or if it's evident you desire to please everyone, they see it as weakness. Leaders love, listen, and look for ways to empower others. But they do so from a position of strength and not weakness. Adversarial women are like sharks in the water. If they smell fear, they will bite. If they have an agenda, they will flatter you to see if they can manipulate you. They look for chinks in your armor, and people-pleasing is a big one. If you are too eager to please for the wrong reasons, they will know and lose respect for you.

> I made a decision. I would not cry again over others' prejudice. Sure, what people thought or said about me might hurt. What people did to me might hurt as well, but I would not carry their narrow-mindedness or bias as my burden . . . I would accomplish all I was capable of. I would concentrate on doing what I believed were the right things for the right reasons to the best of my ability . . . They would not wound me again. I had decided once that my life was my own. Now I decided my heart would be my own as well . . . I have saved my tears for more important things: my family, the beauty of nature, Beethoven, a dear friend, the goodness of people, their wisdom, their tragedies or their triumphs.
>
> **—Carly Fiorina, former CEO of Hewlett-Packard**[16]

PEOPLE-PLEASERS AND CONFLICT

Most people-pleasers will go to any length to avoid conflict. They assume that all conflict is destructive because it includes disagreements and differences. As a result, they run from conflict, allowing it to escalate.

As a new bride, I desperately wanted to be the perfect Christian wife. Not raised in a Christian home, I had no clue what that looked like so I worked from a faulty picture. In my mind, the perfect wife served her family tirelessly, never asked for help, and never complained. Of course, my husband isn't perfect so he would do something to irritate me. But the perfect Christian wife just smiles and stuffs. I bottled up each irritation and insensitive action, until he said or did the one "camel's back" thing, and then I exploded, spewing what I had saved up for months. The escapade usually took all weekend, terminating usual life while I regurgitated my grievances, accompanied by weeping and wailing. My poor husband, a dear man, hardly knew what to do with me.

As I studied the Bible and was mentored by wise women, I learned that my people-pleasing was counterproductive. I learned to express my complaints and irritations in small, appropriate doses. I learned to express myself without overreacting and without hypercharged words and body language. These lessons have served me well in marriage and in ministry.

THE CURE FOR PEOPLE-PLEASING

The cure is simple. Perform for an audience of One. Carly Fiorina writes, "Learning to please God instead of man is the single greatest remedy to the problem of pleasing man . . . the fear of man is to be replaced with the fear of God. The desire to please man above all else is to be replaced with the desire to please God above all else . . . The love of man's approval is to be replaced with the love of God's approval."[17]

What are the advantages of pleasing God instead of people? God is not partial but deals with each of us honestly and justly, regardless of gender, race, or background. God loves us unconditionally and knows we are in process. We don't have to perform for

God's approval. God wants only our best and will not use or abuse us. He is constant so we can trust Him completely. And He knows all things so that as we depend on Him for direction, He won't steer us wrong.

We have learned that when your main concern is pleasing God, you actually please more people. They respect you for your inner strength and your authentic walk with God. Of course, not everyone does, but we will show you ways to limit their damage and take the high road regardless.

FURTHER HELP

Our goal in this book is not to thoroughly diagnose or treat people-pleasing. If you struggle with people-pleasing, consider digesting one or more of the recommended resources in the adjacent box. But get serious about overcoming this fatal flaw in ministry. If you want to make a difference for Jesus, you must eradicate people-pleasing. You can choose to live in the shadows, but if you determine to get on the front lines, conflict awaits. The mandatory skill of peacemaking enables you to survive long term, and even thrive, in ministry.

Additional Resources for People-Pleasers:

Pleasing People by Lou Priolo, Phillipsburg, NJ: P&R Publishing Company, 2007.

The Disease to Please by Harriet Braiker, New York, NY: McGraw-Hill, 2001.

Too Nice for Your Own Good by Duke Robinson, New York, NY: Warner Books, 1997.

Priolo is a Christian author. Braiker and Robinson do not include God in their solutions but nevertheless offer some sound principles.

BULLDOZERS

On the other end of the spectrum from the people-pleaser is the bulldozer. These women are tough, sometimes too tough. Picture a no-nonsense leader. Maybe she is overseeing a staff, or a church picnic, or transportation to a conference. Suddenly, a conflict erupts, and to the bulldozer, it seems silly. These women don't "put up with a lot of guff." When a woman complains that the event was not undergirded with enough prayer, the potato salad was sour, or the bus driver was rude, the bulldozer's response is, "Get a life!"

EASY PREY

Justine accomplished more in a week than many women could in a month. God gifted her with keen intellect, quick wit, and a fast tongue, allowing her to run circles around the women she ministered to and the men she worked with. But these traits sometimes spelled trouble. Her assistant quit out of exhaustion as she tried to implement Justine's many projects. Her students could not keep up. And Justine had little patience with "slow" people. The stage was set for conflict and a couch was the culprit.

Her new office needed furniture but Justine had failed to budget funds to purchase any. So she asked for donations. Margaret, who was redecorating her home, knew the pink floral couch would be perfect in Justine's new office and delivered it herself. Justine was not particular about furniture, but the pink flowers set her teeth on edge, so she left Margaret a message on her answering machine to come and get it. Deeply wounded, Margaret complied but spent the next year raising up a brigade of women to oust Justine. Surely someone as insensitive as Justine should not represent God in His church! Justine might have averted the conflict by taking the time to thank Margaret face-to-face, graciously explaining why the couch would not work. Or she could simply have reupholstered the couch or lived with it and had much less hassle in the long run. After all, Justine asked for donations, a quick but not well-thought-through strategy.

BULLDOZER'S WATERLOO

A bulldozer like Justine is likely to ignore the conflict, determining that it's not worth her time or effort. And she's probably right. What is a floral couch when Bible messages need preparing, affecting women's eternal destinies? But Justine's response plays into the hands of women like Margaret who promptly announce to all her friends that Justine won't listen to the women of the church. Justine doesn't care what other women think. Justine has her own agenda. Certainly Justine should not be leading them.

Bulldozers are easy prey for well-meaning women who create huge problems. Yes, it's infuriating to stop important work for the Lord and deal with these seemingly petty issues. But if you don't, the conflict will probably mushroom and you'll be sorry.

"VELVET-COVERED BRICKS"

John Maxwell calls the best leaders "velvet-covered bricks" —not people-pleasers or bulldozers—strong on the inside but soft on the outside.

Velvet-Covered Brick leaders are not afraid to deal with conflict in order to iron out an unhealthy situation. By actively addressing problems, they are peacemakers as opposed to peacekeepers. At the same time, such a leader remains open to the perspective of others. Although supremely confident, a wise leader knows the fallibility of his or her judgment, and they turn an attentive ear to those who share differing opinions.[18]

Now there is a picture women can relate to! Discard your tendency toward people-pleasing and bulldozing and instead, like Grace, seek to become a "velvet-covered brick."

PRACTICE, PRACTICE, PRACTICE

Do you tend toward people-pleasing or bulldozing? If you fall into one of the extreme categories, you will need to counteract these tendencies and learn to think and act differently not just when the conflict arises, but every day. Skills require practice, and lots of it. Think of something you do well—maybe playing a musical instrument, swinging a tennis racket, or making a pie. You worked long and hard to master this skill. Learning to respond to personal attacks, handle conflict wisely, and understand church politics does not come overnight. You must practice, practice, practice. We suggest that you work on peacemaking in your everyday relationships with family, friends, and coworkers.

Learn the skills incrementally. You can't wait until the first time a woman takes you aside and verbally flays you. Intense emotions will likely take over your good sense and you will respond poorly. Wise women and influential leaders pursue peacemaking skills and wise responses in everyday relationships, adopting sound peacemaking strategies as natural response patterns.

Now may the God of peace who by the blood of the eternal covenant brought back from the dead the great shepherd of the sheep, our Lord Jesus Christ, equip you with every good thing to do his will, working in us what is pleasing before him through Jesus Christ, to whom be glory forever. Amen.

—Hebrews 13:20–21

Discussion *Questions*

1. Why are people-pleasers and bulldozers particularly vulnerable in conflict?

2. To be a successful peacemaker, you must pursue emotional health. What criteria do you use to measure whether or not you are emotionally healthy? How well do you know yourself?

3. Do you struggle with identity issues? Who do you live to please? yourself? others? God? How might your answer affect your actions and attitudes in a conflict?

4. How does pride hinder peacemaking?

5. Review the five characteristics of people-pleasing. Do you see any of these traits in yourself? If so, what can you do to snuff out people-pleasing?

6. List qualities you have observed in women you might describe as bulldozers. Do you struggle with bulldozing? If so, what problems result?

7. What is the cure for people-pleasing? for bulldozing?

Spot Women Who Wound

Chapter 4

Take note of the one who has integrity! Observe the godly!
For the one who promotes peace has a future.

—Psalm 37:37

INTERNSHIP IMPASSE

When Gloria learned Clearwater Community Church approved her required internship, she wanted to "leap like calves released from the stall" as described in her morning devotions in Malachi 4. She drove by this megachurch every morning on her way to seminary, dreaming of an opportunity to learn from children's minister Kate Jaggers. Clearwater was known for its creativity and innovation—qualities she hoped to bring back to her home church in Ohio when she stepped into the children's director position they were holding until she completed her studies. Vivacious, bright, and eager to learn, Gloria arrived dressed in the expected business casual attire and greeted recent recruit Joan, the children's ministry administration assistant.

"Hello, I'm Gloria Adams, I'm the new intern from Dallas Seminary." Gloria extended her hand, looked Joan in the eye, and smiled.

Joan responded with an insipid handshake and two words: "Sit down." Joan stepped back into her office, settled in at her desk, and continued to collate papers and answer email.

Half an hour later, Minister Kate arrived and escorted Gloria into her office, where they spent the morning getting to know each other and envisioning ways Gloria's one-year internship might enhance the children's ministry as well as Gloria's future. Kate invited Gloria to lunch, and on the way, Kate showed Gloria her desk. She would be sharing an office with "Ad man" Joan.

Gloria settled into her duties, connecting with other staff and working extra hours so she could observe and learn as much as possible. She enjoyed long conversations on the phone, her exuberance evident as she laughed and made inquires. Staff and lay leaders, drawn to Gloria, often stopped by the office to visit. Organized and detailed, Joan spent most of her day making sure the supply closet was stocked and workers were in place. Gloria asked Joan about her family and background, with minimal response. Joan was there to work and not chat. Once Gloria asked Joan to help her find some names in the database. "Sorry, dear, interns are not on my job description," was the reply.

One morning, Kate informed Gloria about the three o'clock meeting for that afternoon. The two of them would be joined by Joan and Mike, the executive pastor. Perplexed, Gloria slipped into Kate's office, closed the door, and asked, "What's the meeting about?"

"Well, we need to discuss some issues between you and Joan."

"I didn't know there were any issues between me and Joan. Why didn't she come to me?" asked Gloria, flabbergasted.

"I don't know. Apparently there are, and she didn't bring them to me either. She went straight to Mike."

A tear trickled down Gloria's cheek, streams following. Crazy thoughts ran through Gloria's head. *What had Joan said to Mike? What was Mike thinking? Will word get out? Will this ruin my reputation at the church? Will I ever get a good reference from Mike? What did I do to cause her to complain about me to the executive pastor?*

Kate handed her a tissue, advising her gently, "Gloria, we will work this out. You've done great work and your attitude has been stellar. These things happen in ministry. I want you to go down to the prayer room to pray and pull yourself together. I'll be praying here."

When Gloria returned at three o'clock, Mike had already

arrived and Joan was sitting in the corner, steel-faced. After some small talk, Mike prayed and then addressed the accuser. "Joan, I understand that you have some issues with Gloria and this is your opportunity to voice your thoughts and feelings so we can work through the situation."

Joan glared at Gloria. "I don't feel comfortable talking about this and I have nothing to say." Later Gloria learned that Joan had no idea Mike would bring the two women face-to-face. In her corporate experience, open dialogue was not part of conflict resolution. In her old job, her boss would have made note of the complaint, and Gloria probably would not have had an opportunity to respond. Welcome to Matthew 18, Joan.

What happened next surprised Gloria as much as anybody. She leaned toward Joan and said, "Joan, obviously there are problems between us. But we are sisters in Christ and I would like to hear what they are so I can work on them. I want us to be able to work together but I can't improve if I don't understand the problem. However, I would appreciate your coming straight to me. I promise to listen and try to work it out." Joan sat silent.

For Gloria, the rest of the meeting was a blur. She had asked God to calm her emotions in the prayer room and He had, at least outwardly. But in spite of her gentle response, she felt shredded on the inside. Mike finished the meeting with some good words. He prayed, and encouraged the women to work on their differences, but everyone left with a sense that little had been accomplished, except that Joan learned that her going-behind-the-back-of-her-boss strategy did not work at Clearwater.

As they were leaving, Kate pulled Gloria back into her office and closed the door. "I am so proud of you. I know this hurt, but you handled it very well. Welcome to ministry."

A few days later, Gloria approached Joan again, asking for honesty and friendship. Joan replied, "This is my job. I am here to work and I'm not looking for friends. I have plenty of friends already."

The rest of the year Gloria and Joan coexisted in an icy silence. Gloria kept her phone conversations and personal visits to a minimum, wondering if that might be the source of the problem. Her last day she thanked Kate for all she had learned. She reflected, "I left sad that the internship was over, but glad that I will never have to walk into the office I shared with Joan again." Gloria wondered as she walked away if ministry was really for her. Had she somehow brought this situation on herself? Those questions haunted her for years.

Gloria learned a hard and priceless lesson. Sometimes as much as you try, if the other party is unwilling, you cannot make peace. Sometimes the conflict turns destructive, no matter what you do. In this chapter, we will look at the difference between constructive and destructive conflict, and we will learn ways to identify characteristics of women who won't make peace.

Gloria handled the situation well, especially with so little ministry experience. But she allowed Joan to shut down her excitement, coloring her memory of the internship. Joan was not a healthy woman, and she did not continue at Clearwater for much longer. But had Gloria been able to understand the kind of woman she was dealing with, she might have been able to walk away without blaming or doubting herself.

WELCOME CONSTRUCTIVE CRITICISM

When atheist Sam Harris wrote his 2004 bestseller *The End of Faith*, a radical attack on religious beliefs in any form, he was prepared for strong rebuttals from Christians. What may have surprised him was the vitriol in which many of the emails and letters were couched. The most hostile messages came from Christians (not Muslims or Hindus). "The truth is," he explained in the foreword to his latest bestseller, *Letter to a Christian Nation*, "that many who claim to be transformed by God's love are deeply, even murderously, intolerant of criticism." "How do I know this?" he asked rhetorically. "The most disturbed of my correspondence always cite chapter and verse."[1]

We understand why Christians reacted to Harris' attack, but hateful responses only played into his hands, making an excellent foreword to his next book. Whether our critic is right or wrong, if our response is defensive or caustic, we hinder the peace process and dishonor our Lord.

We all need correcting. We all battle pride and we all make mistakes, need attitude adjustments, and lose perspective. One measure of our spiritual maturity is whether or not we are open to hearing words of instruction.

> Do not rebuke a mocker or he will hate you;
> rebuke a wise man and he will love you.
> Instruct a wise man and he will be wiser still;
> teach a righteous man and he will add to his learning.
> Proverbs 9:8–9 NIV

Constructive criticism is designed to help us grow and minister more effectively. Can you welcome caring confrontation delivered with kindness and a desire to help? For people-pleasers and perfectionists, it still hurts to be told we are not measuring up. But there are worse things than feeling hurt—like reacting poorly to a rebuke and becoming embroiled in out-of-control conflict. Gloria was deeply hurt, but she took those emotions to the Lord, and He helped her respond constructively. God can do the same for any of us.

So swallow your pride and woundedness, grab hold of those emotions, and respond to a rebuke with wise words. If ambushed, you might say, "You could be right" or "I will consider what you have said and get back to you." If you find yourself invited to a surprise meeting like Gloria did, put aside what you are doing and get with God. Implore Him to help you respond graciously and biblically. Then enter into the conflict resolution process committed to honor God and build up your critic.

Most critics are normal, healthy people who are displeased or hurt and need attention. They need to know that you care about them and that you will listen to their ideas. Become a skilled peacemaker so you will know what to do and say, raising the likelihood that the issue ends well for everyone—and most of the time it does. The following chapters will help you become an expert, if you apply what you learn and make it a lifestyle. But sometimes constructive turns destructive.

BEWARE DESTRUCTIVE CRITICISM

Sometimes your critic isn't normal or healthy, like Joan. Or sometimes a normal healthy critic treated badly, ignored, or disrespected, like Dr. Jeckel and Mr. Hyde, rapidly transforms into an unrecognizable dragon.[2] Every situation is different. The conflict between Gloria and Joan was a short-lived personality clash, but often conflicts escalate to damage more than a young woman's internship.

Somebody wants something. The major complication is that the issues at the core (personal and selfish desires) get communicated as if they are the cause of Christ. This is not new. Holy wars have been fought with the same dynamics in play. This is further complicated because it's rarely malice that drives the personal agenda. It's more often good people who really believe what they are doing (what they want) is right. The problem is that good people who are attempting to do good things lose sight of the big picture and begin to justify their part of the mission as The Mission. When the situation reaches the state where it does become ugly and wars begin, all perspective is lost and we (after the fact) hear stories of things that happen in local churches that we can hardly believe are true . . . the church is tremendously wounded. God's heart is crushed and Christianity gets another black eye.[3]

Our goal is to keep the conflict from escalating into a war, if possible. We nip it in the bud. Part of our task as a skilled peacemaker is to figure out who we are dealing with as soon as possible.

Don't label your adversary as unhealthy too quickly. If you do the reconciliation process will be colored by this assumption. Communications expert Barbara Pachter has conducted more than thirteen hundred skill-building seminars on topics including conflict resolution. She cautions us:

> If you approach a confrontation thinking, "Wow! What a jerk!" you may be setting yourself up for a negative experience. If we've decided that someone is a jerk, that means we think he or she has treated us badly, unfairly, unjustly—feelings we don't like. You can easily end up in the land of aggression when you're upset. But if you approach a confrontation thinking, "Maybe this person is a jerk. Maybe not. I'll find out what I'm dealing with first," you are far more likely to have a positive experience.[4]

And often it's not easy. Sometimes our critic is a normal, healthy person who we push over the edge by our neglect or foolish responses. Sometimes our critic was a "wolf in a spiritual sheep's clothing" all along. We may never know.

The end result is the same—we are dealing with an unreasonable, unhealthy person who is determined to destroy us and the ministry. Remember they don't believe this about themselves. They justify their actions and wholeheartedly believe they are doing God's work, which makes them all the more dangerous. How can you tell if you are embroiled in a destructive conflict with an unhealthy adversary?

People both appreciate and resent strength and success in others; for the same reasons, strong, successful people are both admired and attacked. Some people see inspiration for themselves in others' success. Some people who think they cannot accomplish their objectives alone ally themselves with strong people when their goals and agendas are aligned. Some people who are equally strong and successful, may choose open confrontation if they disagree, but they do so with real respect. And some people simply resent others' strength because it highlights their own perceived inadequacies. Some are jealous of success they see as greater than their own. Jealousy and resentment are feelings of inferiority and

*inadequacy, and they breed resistance and the instinct to engage
in an unfair fight.[5]*

CHARACTERISTICS OF UNHEALTHY
WOMEN WHO WOUND

1. Adversarial

Watch out for women who are itching for a fight. They love
to pick arguments and enjoy controversy. Charlotte told me,
"That's just the way we communicate in our family." When invited into her home, I witnessed arguing, bantering, and sarcasm
firsthand. I wasn't surprised when Charlotte brought her con-
tentiousness and complaining into the ministry.

> **I have often wondered**, that persons who make boast of
> professing the Christian religion, namely love, joy, peace,
> temperance, and charity to all men, should quarrel with
> such rancorous animosity, and display daily towards one
> another such bitter hatred, that this, rather than the virtues
> which they claim, is the readiest criteria of their faith.[6]
>
> **—Benedict de Spinoza, Jewish philosopher**

2. Old guard

Typically, as a church grows, some people who were there
first resent new people and the leaders who bring them in. These
dissenters are known as the "old guard." They disguise their irritation with spiritual-sounding arguments like, "The church is so
big that nobody knows anybody anymore. This is not the way
God wants our church to be." If their social world has been disturbed and now they lack power, they will fight to keep the status
quo. These gripers are more concerned with their own social status than with people's eternal destiny. Fortunately not everyone

who founded the church acts this way, but enough do that they have been branded with this name and reputation.

When I was hired as minister to women, Old Guard Denise let me know that she was the unofficial guardian of the women's ministry. Hired in from the outside, my first task was to spend individual time with influential women of the church. Denise made it clear that this was "her church." And she explained that God had given her the gift of prophecy, which she interpreted as putting her on the same plane as Isaiah or Ezekiel. Like an Old Testament prophet, she saw her role as God's instrument to ensure I did not veer "to the right or to the left." (More stories about Denise later.)

3. Tunnel vision

God gifts each woman differently, and all our gifts are needed to create a balanced ministry that represents Christ well. But if a woman is unbalanced emotionally, she may be skewed in her thinking about what ministry should look like. For example, if she has the gift of evangelism, an unbalanced woman will expect the entire ministry to be about evangelism. If she is called to minister to the inner city, she will become angry when resources go overseas. She has a narrow special interest and, through her unhealthy, clouded vision, you are a bad leader, a "villain", if you don't make her agenda your agenda.

4. Intense

The women who have wounded me the most were initially my strongest supporters. Intense women care passionately about God's work, but if they are unhealthy, these intense feelings are often misguided. One of my "dragons" made an appointment soon after I arrived. With a kowtowing attitude, and oozing flattery, she offered her friendship and services in any area of the ministry where I might need her, day or night. Naïve, I was elated. I needed committed workers and she seemed perfect. *Lord, give me an army of women like this!* I immediately drafted her onto my leadership team. BIG mistake! Initially, she worked hard but later turned on me and attempted to ruin my reputation and effectiveness.

A beloved Dallas Seminary professor, Dr. Stan Toussaint, tells his students, "Beware the man who meets you at the train." Be wary of the overenthusiastic welcoming committee of one.

Dragons often work overhard initially at befriending you. If you list the people who make an appointment to see you in the first month of a new pastorate and another list of those unhappy with your ministry a year later, you'll be amazed at the overlap. Often when they first come, they want to "share a personal concern" or let you know "the real situation in the church." They really want, of course, to co-opt your allegiance for their special interest.[7]

These intense women are often overgenerous with money if they have any, sometimes attempting to "buy" favors that result in them getting their way. A husband of one of my dragons offered a million dollars toward a building project if the senior pastor would favor his wife over me in a conflict. Thankfully, the pastor recognized a bribe when he saw one and did not succumb.

5. Super-spiritual

Watch out for unhealthy women who spiritualize everything. They don't seem to be able to talk in normal English. Everything is "God told me . . . " and "God doesn't want it done this way." When I made the decision to leave church ministry for the academy, I announced my intentions publicly at Bible study. Soon afterward, a woman who had earned her reputation as a troublemaker, made an appointment to see me. In the meeting she announced that "God told me that I am to take your place."

I was shocked. This woman had caused incredible problems in our ministry and for the male staff. She would be the last woman hired to replace me. Trying to respond kindly, I asked, "Why do you want to oversee this ministry?" She replied, "Oh, *I* don't want your job. *God* wants me to do this."

Beware of super-spiritual language that disguises power plays and fleshly attitudes. Sick women can learn how to manipulate others using spiritual language to gain the upper hand. Often, they don't even know what they are doing. And, if you are not alert, they can fool you. Of course, some women who seem super-spiritual really are that way. You have to discern whether they are authentic or just playing games—and often that takes time and keen senses. Don't be too quick to place women in positions of authority. Be sure they are the real deal, honest, teachable, and humble. Super-spirituality may be a mask to cover up immaturity, hurt, or pathology.

6. Blind

Unhealthy adversaries can't see the damage they do. As a result, they refuse to take responsibility. Cybil was the church gossip, which she justified by naming herself the go-to woman. In her mind, she knew and cared deeply for everybody in the church. She voted herself unofficial "mother of the church" and, in her mind, this position gave her license to delve into everyone's lives and fix everyone's problems. But her gossip was wrapped in indirect aggression—the kinds that we learned about in Chapter Two. She was an expert at coating her malicious talk in sugary rhetoric to cover the reality that she was a nosy busybody. Her meddling was the source of multiple problems in the church.

Finally, the elders had enough and called her in to an elders' meeting. As a woman on staff, I was asked to attend with her. The elders methodically presented examples of her gossip, word for word, as well as problems she had caused. I was embarrassed for her, and if I had been her, I would have wanted to dig a hole in the floor and never show my face in the church again. But afterward, as we were leaving, she turned to me and said, "I just don't see how I could have done anything different." I was struck by the reality that she did not see the damage she was doing.

I'm amazed at the way sickness can cloud perception. This blindness is the reason why some of these conflicts go on and on and on. In the face of reason and rebuke, unhealthy women often cannot see the damage they do. They persist in their "holy crusade," unaware that people's lives are scorched and God's name is blackened.

7. Frustrated

Troublemaking women are usually frustrated women. Marshall Shelley explains, "Dragons often sensed a call to ministry at one time. Surprisingly, most pastors indicate they do not have as many problems with those currently in Christian work as they do with those who should be in ministry but aren't . . . The problems come from those who've sensed a call and haven't followed it. It's the frustrated armchair pastors who want to run the church."[8]

Women who want to make a difference for the Lord but are hindered because of family responsibilities, lack of courage, financial limitations, or feelings of inferiority sometimes take their frustrations out on women who are doing what they want to do. It's so easy to be an expert until you are in the midst of ministry. People who criticize leaders are often people who have never led anything and have no clue what is involved. But in their inflated and unhealthy minds, they have all the answers.

BE ON GUARD

When I observe women with any of the above qualities, I'm on guard. They are not necessarily dragons but they could be. Watch for further signs. For example, Lydia, an influential woman in the church, exhibited several of these characteristics. She was old guard, super-spiritual, and intense. She darted from project to project with a fire that quickly cooled. She made rash decisions—instead of dieting to take off a few extra pounds, she had plastic surgery. Living on a tight budget, she cashed in her 401K and bought a top-of-the-line motorcycle. Bizarre stuff—red flags. I was right. She later caused terrible problems in the ministry.

If you lead a ministry, take your time bringing women into your inner leadership circle. If you work as a lay volunteer, be careful whom you choose as your partner. Conflict is part of ministry. Expect it. Understand it. Become an expert peacemaker. One skill you must master is the ability to identify whether the conflict is constructive or destructive—and whether you are dealing with a normal healthy critic or a pink dragon. The conflict resolution process will be similar. However, when you know your adversary is unhealthy, you are more guarded, more realistic in your expectations, and more careful to protect yourself.

UNDERSTAND YOUR ADVERSARY

Why do women criticize and attack? We can't see inside a woman's head and heart. In some cases we will never know her motivation or even her mental health. Be careful not to classify a woman as unhealthy too quickly, something unhealthy women will probably do to you. Dragons judged me to be a "demon" almost immediately. We must not make the same mistake. Take into account these factors as you assess an adversary.

1. Gift-mix

Spiritual gifts like teaching, wisdom, and prophecy carry with them tendencies toward black-and-white thinking. These women see error or injustice and embark on a correction crusade. They struggle to be compassionate and merciful. They can be blunt in their communication style. Their timing is often insensitive.

Rival Bible teacher Sylvia barged into Bible study a few minutes before I was slated to teach. Did she realize that her timing was unkind? I doubt it. I think she was oblivious. Nevertheless, in front of several leaders, she confronted me on a theological point on which we differed, shouting and pointing her finger in my face. I explained that I was preparing to lecture and could we please talk about this some other time. She stomped out.

Adrenaline racing, composure shaken, I fought to regain equilibrium so I could focus to teach the three hundred expectant students. I believe Sylvia is an example of a gifted woman who had not worked to overcome extremist tendencies in her life. Her gift-mix was all hard side. As a result, she told her students, "I'm not here to be your friend. I'm here to teach you the Bible." As you can imagine, her students' attendance waned over the course.

To help understand gifts, I categorize them into two groups—hard side and soft side. Women with hard side gifts (teaching, wisdom, prophecy) tend to be more factual, goal-oriented bottom-liners, lacking in compassion. Women with soft side gifts (encouragement, mercy) tend to make excuses for people. With each gift-mix set there are tremendous strengths, but there are also weaknesses. Some women are endowed with both hard side and soft side gifts, and they are not in as much danger of extremes. But for those of us with a one-sided gift mix, we have to be aware and work hard not to become like Sylvia.

2. Background and past experiences

Our past experiences shape us, as well as our innate qualities. Women who have not processed their pain continue to carry it. Hurt women hurt women. That's good to know but that doesn't lessen the pain they inflict.

> **In the church**, most dragons see themselves as godly people, adequately gracious and kind, who hold another viewpoint they honestly believe is right. Unfortunately *sincerity without self-examination is no excuse.* Remember the old joke about the proud mother who thought every member of the marching band was out of step except her Freddy?[9] (emphasis ours)
>
> —**Marshall Shelley**
> *Well-Intentioned Dragons*

Troublemaking women often wound out of complex personal backgrounds. Wounded women may continue to criticize you and your ministry, not because they are actually upset about issues, but because they are mad at you. You have ignored or neglected them in some way. You remind them of their great-aunt Sarah. Or they have problems with authority figures. Their demands may be unreasonable but their feelings are real.

One of my adversaries was a white witch before she came to faith. Another grew up in an oppressive legalistic home and was molested by a physician as a girl. Understanding a woman's pain may help us respond with compassion, but we cannot excuse her behavior. Encourage women to do the hard work of becoming emotionally healthy. Refer these women to caring professional therapists if their problems are deep and complex—because although a conflict with a wounded woman may begin as constructive, it can quickly transition into a malicious situation.

3. Subjective knowers

In the mid-eighties, four women scholars conducted a study that explained different kinds of female learners.[10] Their findings help us understand how women make decisions, perceive themselves, overcome obstacles, and interact with others. Almost half of the women studied turned out to be "subjective knowers." These women make decisions on the basis of their "gut" or intuition, on how they feel. These women are antirational, completely subjective, and dependent on emotions. Cynical and suspicious, most of these women do not trust authority figures. Many are wounded women who reject all knowledge from outside sources, again trusting only their "gut."

With half of women classified as subjective knowers, we can expect to find many in the church. How might subjective knowers interact in a conflict? Based on the above qualities, not well.

This type of woman is unlikely to consider that she may be wrong. Controlled by her emotions, she may be unreasonable. Already disliking authority, she may be biased toward anyone in a leadership role. If we find ourselves face-to-face with a subjective knower as an opponent, we need to be sure we take the time to process the emotional aspects of the dispute. We also need to understand that if, in her gut, she feels you are wrong or bad, you may soon be dealing with a dragon.

4. The flesh

And, of course, we can't forget the flesh, as we discussed in Chapter Two. We are all in-process sinners, in different degrees of refinement, guaranteeing conflict and strife in our relationships. You and I are not free of the flesh, which Paul describes as "hatred, discord, jealousy, fits of rage, selfish ambition, dissentions, factions and envy."[11] You won't respond like Gloria in every situation and neither will your adversary. You may find you make progress and then a new situation erupts, providing a new chance to blow it. Becoming a peacemaking woman is a long, hard process. But it's mandatory if you want your life to count for Christ.

SO FAR . . .

We looked at the cause and complexities of conflict. We challenged you to alter your assumptions and expect women who wound. We've gleaned lessons from secular studies on ways women in the world wound one another, as well as gender differences in conflict styles. We asked you to take an honest look in the mirror, particularly at areas that make you vulnerable in conflict.

In this chapter, we attempted to discern the differences between constructive and destructive conflict, hoping to prepare you for real situations. And we identified seven different characteristics of unhealthy women, looking also at reasons for their dysfunction. In the pages ahead, we will discover specific strategies to enable us to survive and even thrive among women who wound.

But avoid foolish controversies, genealogies, quarrels, and fights about the law, because they are useless and empty. Reject a divisive person after one or two warnings. You know that such a person is twisted by sin and is conscious of it himself.

—Titus 3:9–11

Discussion *Questions*

1. How would you differentiate between constructive and destructive criticism?

2. Review the seven characteristics of unhealthy women who wound. Have you observed these qualities in women you know? (No names, please.)

3. Do you observe any of these qualities in yourself? If so, what can you do to ensure that you don't become a "dragon" to others?

4. How can our gift-mix cause us to be a destructive critic?

5. What is a "subjective knower"? Why are these women difficult to deal with in conflict?

6. Why is it important that we develop the ability to discern between emotionally healthy and unhealthy critics? How does this knowledge affect the way we proceed in resolving conflict?

7. Have you ever been attacked by a "dragon"? How did you handle the conflict and what did you learn? (No names. Please use caution to protect the identity of anyone involved.)

Disarm Women Who Wound

Chapter 5

I give you a new commandment—to love one another.
Just as I have loved you, you also are to love one another.
Everyone will know by this that you are my disciples—
if you have love for one another.

—John 13:34–35

ROCKS AND FIRECRACKERS

The kids' fourth of July celebration blew up more than their illegal fireworks. The noise infuriated a neighbor who came outside to confront the youngsters. Tempers flared and the alleged assailant went back inside his apartment, returned with a handgun, and shot nineteen-year-old Broderick Gains in the head. After the ambulance sped away, an angry crowd threw rocks into the shooter's window followed by lit firecrackers, setting the apartment on fire.[1] Turn on the evening news to view out-of-control violence every night.

NUNS WITH ROCKS

In a previously serene Italian convent, a group of nuns assaulted their Mother Superior, who required hospital treatment for scratches to her face. The nuns apparently had been chafing for months under the heavy-handed rule of their victim and decided enough was enough. The senior nun has asked the pope to come to her aid in the insurrection.[2]

STICKS AND STONES IN THE CITY COUNCIL

Taxpayers in Ashland, Oregon, will pay $37,000 for five months of conflict counseling for their city council. The catalyst was when one councilman told another to "shut your —— mouth" during a council meeting. The week before, the victim verbally attacked the mayor, calling him a "Nazi." City Administrator Martha Bennett admitted that $37,000 may "seem like a lot of money, but if the council doesn't function, the city doesn't function."[3]

Christians don't usually throw rocks, burn down apartments, shoot one another in the head, hospitalize their superiors, or require group counseling. But the damage to God's work is equally destructive. How can we learn to lay down our rocks?

LEARNING THE HARD WAY

I came to faith through a parachurch women's Bible study. For more than fifteen years, the leaders re-parented and trained me, transforming my life. When our founder retired, I was asked to oversee the recruitment and training of the teaching team. In my mid-thirties, I was green and overwhelmed, but eager to learn and lead. My first test came in the form of a conflict and I failed miserably.

David Johnson writes, "It is not the presence of conflict that causes chaos and disaster, but the harmful and ineffective way it is managed. It is the lack of skills in managing conflict that leads to problems. When conflicts are skillfully managed, they are of value."[4]

The opposite is also true. When conflicts are badly managed, they are damaging. In my first test, I lacked the skills to manage conflict effectively, resulting in everyone's hurt feelings.

A SEASON OF REGRET

Twenty-eight-year-old Sarah wanted to join the teaching team, which was by invitation only. She was married to a prominent man in the community and her father was a distinguished pastor, known for his preaching expertise. Attractive, witty, and intelligent, she worked as a trainer in corporate America before joining the Bible study. Almost immediately, we invited her into the leader's group and, within a year, I heard rumblings that she expected me to invite her to teach.

Her indirect request struck me as impertinent, irritating me from the beginning. Looking back, I now realize that I felt she was trying to ride on Daddy's coattails when everyone else had to earn their own way on merit—namely me. My father was deceased, my husband was an engineer, and no one else in my family was in ministry. Maybe there was a little jealousy on my part. But back then I did not know myself well enough to be that discerning.

Naïve and insecure, I went by the rules—and the rules said that in our Bible study, teachers were chosen by invitation only. However, this was a unique situation. Sarah was influential, and the ministry would benefit if her father lent us his name, more likely if his daughter was a Bible teacher. Of course, no one voiced this reality out loud, but I felt pressure to bend the rules for the good of the study. Resentful, I bowed to politics and made an appointment with Sarah.

We met over lunch, where I laid out the process. A teacher-apprentice began as a guest lecturer in another teacher's series, allowing for a mentoring relationship. The mentor worked with the apprentice, reviewing her messages and offering suggestions to help her refine her teaching skills. I taught periodic workshops that Sarah would be required to attend. When we felt she was ready, she would choose a book of the Bible to teach, prepare curriculum and lectures, and join the circuit, all overseen by more experienced teachers. She listened intently and seemed amenable. We parted and I expected her to embark on the process.

However, I began to hear indirectly that Sarah was complaining to other leaders with comments like, "No one else has to jump through all these hoops." The accusation was not true, but obviously she felt I was treating her unfairly. I was furious. I had been coerced into the offer and now she wasn't willing to submit to the training process. And instead of voicing these objections to

me directly she was complaining to other leaders, causing dis-
sention in the ranks!

I knew what to do—it was time for Matthew 18. I asked Janet
to join me on a campaign to show Sarah the error of her ways.
Janet and I shared leadership of the study—she over administration and me over teaching. I asked her to set up a time when the
three of us could meet. Unfortunately, all our calendars were full
for three weeks—so the meeting was scheduled a month out.
When Sarah asked why we were meeting, Janet explained there
were some problems we needed to discuss. Sarah now had a whole
month to worry.

The meeting was unproductive. First, Sarah asked why we
waited so long to meet. For her, the last month had been torture,
her imagination running wild. She was in tears from the beginning. I quickly apologized for the timing, but, despite her tears, my
words were seasoned with my irritation. With so much manipulation before, I felt manipulated again. I don't remember the details—just the atmosphere—tense. For more than an hour we
bantered back and forth, trying to communicate but never really
connecting, with deep resentment and lack of trust permeating
our words. In the end, together we decided that she would not
enter the apprentice process, a relief to me. I did not believe that
she was ready nor, under the circumstances, did I want to train
her. Playing politics irked me and the decision seemed right. However, I knew that I had failed as a leader. The process was painful,
flawed, and ugly. All three of us limped away, wounded, but I was
primarily responsible. Sarah was wrong but the blame was ultimately mine.

THE CHALLENGE OF GOOD COMMUNICATION

Our goal as skilled peacemakers is to disarm our adversary.
To disarm means to persuade another to lay down their inclina-
tion to be hostile, so we can talk—really talk. Good communication occurs when two people are open, honest, vulnerable,
transparent, and looking for ways for both to benefit. Poor communication results when two people are defensive, threatened,

fearful of being misunderstood, protective, hiding behind masks, worried about making an impression, and wanting to win.

Good communication is a skill, a combination of using the right words, listening intently, and getting feedback to ensure we are not misunderstood. And that's just the verbal side. The non-verbal, facial expressions, body language, voice intonation, emotional overtones, eye contact, are also powerful communicators. No wonder skilled communicators are rare!

When we are interacting with people we love and trust, healthy communication is more likely, although even then we experience challenges. But when we are interacting with an adversary, the opportunity for misunderstandings and harmful outcomes increases. Then add to the mix that women tend to extend the conflict beyond the actual disagreement—both in their personal application and their tendency to form supportive coalitions. Throw in the emotional component and you have the makings of a disaster. No wonder women's conflict so often ends badly!

PUT DOWN YOUR ROCK FIRST

Only committed peacemakers can navigate the stormy sea of conflict. A first step is to disarm your adversary. How? As a leader, you need to put down your rock first. When you disarm, your opponent may also. But there are no guarantees. One way to distinguish between healthy and unhealthy adversaries is that the former will ultimately put her rock down too, and she will not pick it up again. A dragon may refuse to lay down her rock. Or she may pretend to put it down, but continue the conflict after it looks like it is resolved.

You may need to lay down your rock more than once for your adversary to trust you enough to be willing to lay hers down too. I never said this was easy. But you must try. Because by laying down your rock, you dramatically increase the possibility of healthy dialogue, making resolution possible. Let's look at strategies that show your adversary that you are laying down your rock and inviting her to do the same.

GOOD LESSONS FROM A BAD EXAMPLE

1. Be self-aware

I know we already emphasized the importance of accurate self-perception, but we can't repeat this enough. If I had known myself better, the conflict with Sarah might have turned out differently. Looking back, I see how much my irritation stemmed from my jealousy over her big-name family, and the lack I felt. True, Sarah was pushy to nominate herself as a Bible teacher, but I had already colored my attitude toward her simply because of her impressive roots. Did she expect special treatment or use her background to her advantage? Honestly, I don't remember. I just know that my heart attitude was not Christlike, affecting my tone of voice and nonverbal communication. Women can read between the words. We can feel the emotions behind the intent and it colors how we respond. Prejudice against those we envy is sinful. Had I been more aware I could have prayed for a different attitude, a request Jesus would have granted I'm sure.

2. Be kind

My grandchildren were running in circles when one decided to reverse direction, causing multiple tumbles and a few bruises. After dusting herself off, three-year-old Becca, with hands on hips, confronted the culprit with a hearty, "Be kind!" Good advice for peacemakers. Consider these examples.

Timing is critical. With Sarah, we set ourselves up for failure before we ever met. The timing was cruel. Had we been kind we would have rearranged our calendars and addressed the issue as soon as we were emotionally and spiritually prepared. Sarah was already wounded when she arrived and we were insensitive to make her wait so long. Conflict is emotionally charged, thus deserving top priority regardless of the inconvenience.

We also show kindness by refusing to use our clout to gain an advantage. For example, we choose the meeting place together rather than "my office" where I feel in charge and you may feel intimidated.

Want to demolish trust? Go behind your opponent's back and

meet with a superior on the sly. When I was overseeing a large women's ministry, I was called unexpectedly into the pastor's office. He was the man I reported to on staff. Earlier that week, I had a disagreement with a woman on my team, but we had plans to work out our differences. But before we could, she went to the pastor and unloaded. I was not there to hear what she said or weigh in on any distortions. As a result I was blindsided. The pastor reprimanded me when he did not know the whole story. I sat there dumbfounded, resentment building as I tried to decipher his perceptions of the issue. I left feeling betrayed. I had not even picked up a rock but my opponent had pummeled me with a slew of them before we even talked. I found it terribly difficult to trust her ever again.

*Laying down our rock means we walk in our adversary's shoes. Common kindness goes a long way in disarming an adversary.

3. Don't assume

Women make assumptions that turn out not to be true. I know because I am one of them. I, like many women, am intuitive. I spend inordinate amounts of time trying to figure out relational intricacies. If you want to know how my family is faring emotionally, don't ask my husband. He won't have a clue. Ask me. I pick up on little things—body language, facial expressions, and innuendoes. Since I have this ability, I easily make assumptions in conflicts, especially concerning motivation.

I assumed that Sarah's bold request to be a Bible teacher stemmed from her celebrity status; the prima donna (princess) was used to special privileges, entitlement. And maybe I was right. But I might have been wrong, and I never gave Sarah an opportunity to explain herself. She may not have understood that we selected teachers by invitation only. The women who reported her comments to me may have misrepresented her. Don't ever assume you can trust secondhand, indirect communication. Always sit down face-to-face and seek honest answers. Assumptions are dangerous, often causing women to wound one another over misconceptions.

Other people's intentions exist only in their hearts and minds. They are invisible to us. However real and right our assumptions about other people's intentions may seem to us, they are often incomplete or just plain wrong . . . We assume the worst. The conclusions we draw about intentions based on the impact of others' actions on us are rarely charitable. When a friend shows up late to a movie, we don't think, "Gee, I'll bet he ran into someone in need." More likely we think, "Jerk. He doesn't care about making me miss the beginning of the movie." When we've been hurt by someone else's behavior, we assume the worst.[5]

After jumping to flawed conclusions, the next step is to assume we are dealing with a bad person.

We settle into judgments about their character that color our view of them and, indeed, affect not only any conversation we might have, but the entire relationship. Once we think we have someone figured out, we see all of their actions through that lens, and the stakes rise. Even if we don't share our view with them, the impact remains. The worse our view of the other person's character, the easier it is to justify avoiding them or saying nasty things behind their back.[6]

We must limit the conflict to the facts, the way men usually do. We must allow women the opportunity to explain themselves.

We must also realize that women act and react over a variety of reasons that have nothing to do with us. These women may or may not be aware of their own motivation, just as I was unaware of my prejudice toward Sarah. Too often we assume that our adversary's motivation is personal. They don't like us or something we did or did not do—and it may be true. But there are many other possible reasons. We are smart to *depersonalize* a conflict as much as we can, understanding that the conflict may have little to do with us personally—or if it does, it may be something we cannot or should not change. For example:

- They may be in the midst of an emotional crisis (divorce, runaway teen, job loss)
- They may not agree with you on women's roles and feel you are not representing their view properly
- They may see you as a roadblock for something they want
- They may be angry at someone else and you remind them of that person
- They may expect something from you that you cannot or will not give them
- They may have put you on a pedestal and learned you are only human
- They may fear you will make changes that will decrease their power
- They may be taking prescription medication that makes them unreasonable or irritable
- They may be mentally ill (personality disorders, neurosis, psychosis)
- They may abuse and be under the influence of drugs or alcohol
- They may be jealous of your position or strengths
- They may want your job

Many of these motivations are irrational, meaning your adversary probably won't lay down her rock when you do. But assumptions fuel irrational fires. Stick to the facts for a better shot at healthy communication.

4. Seek points of agreement

In conflict, you may be right but lose anyway. In poorly handled, long-term conflict everyone walks away dirty—especially God's reputation. As a leader, one way to show your adversary that you desire to lay down your rock is to seek points of agreement.

I could have earnestly agreed with Sarah that the timing of

our meeting was unkind instead of waterskiing over the mistake. I could have been more sympathetic when she cried, instead of assuming manipulation. I might have tried to explain to her the rationale for our training process, seeking her understanding. When you go out of your way to be agreeable, you show you are willing to lay down your rock.

5. Create a caring ethos

Every place has an ethos. What is ethos? It's the distinguishing tone, environment, or climate—and it's powerful. It influences how people feel, act, and respond. Maybe you were searching for a church home and you visited church after church—and it just wasn't right. And then you visited a church and it wasn't long before you knew—this is it! You weren't sure why, but you felt at home.

When my (Kelley's) dating relationship fell apart a few months after my boyfriend introduced me to a fantastic but small church, I had to choose—stay in this community where everyone knew what happened and where I'd see my now ex-boyfriend often, or find a new church home and start over. I chose to stay because I realized I had found a place that was worth more than the short-term hurt. They had become my faith family. That is ethos.

Every home has an ethos. Some of us were blessed to be born into families where we were cherished, even when we messed up. Others of us knew we were one breath away from words (or hands) that hurt, no matter how hard we tried. One is an incubator; the other a deep freeze. The first conjures up warm feelings throughout life that energize their offspring. Children from the deep freeze spend much of their life thawing out and trying to overcome the cold. It has nothing to do with the place's material value or its size. It is something intangible, yet of great consequence—it is ethos.

Every classroom has an ethos, whether it's located in a school, church, or living room. The physical room may look almost identical but the teacher or leader sets an atmosphere that profoundly affects what happens there.

And your meeting place has an ethos. All parties involved in the conflict create the ethos. Your goal is to create an ethos that disarms your opponent. Seek a meeting place that will put your adversary at ease. Arrange the furniture so you can sit face-to-face without a large desk separating you. Monitor your tone of voice and body language. Disarm your enemy to the best of your ability.

6. Give your adversary all the time and space she needs

Women carry their hearts into a conflict and need time to talk through their feelings in depth—which to some people means ad nauseum. Some of us are bottom-liners and are quick to say what we think and feel. But many women want to tell every detail, and some process their emotions as they speak. Some women are more articulate than others. Give women who struggle to express themselves adequate opportunity. Show them you really do want to understand what they mean by feeding back what you heard to see if your assessment is accurate. Ask for clarification gently. Don't shut them down by expressing irritation if they are not as quick as you with words.

Resolving conflict is so critical to ministry health that wise women bite the bullet and listen intently for the long haul. Don't schedule other appointments right afterward. Give yourself plenty of time. With women you may be there two or three hours. If you see that exhaustion has set in and you really aren't making progress, you may want to schedule another meeting together soon.

7. Never attempt to resolve conflict in writing

Cowards create conflict through email or online. Refuse to enter into a written exchange. Email is great to set up a meeting but it's flawed and dangerous as a conflict communication medium. First, with a touch of a key, it can draw in people who should not be involved. Second, it's easy to misinterpret email. You can't see the eyes of your adversary or pick up on the emotions, all helpful in diagnosis of the issue and resolving the disagreement. You miss the opportunity to disarm your adversary when you interact electronically.

When someone sends me a conflict-laden email, I stop immediately and respond with instructions on how they can reach me in person should they desire to discuss the issue, and I delete anonymous emails without reading them. If they don't have the courage to sign their names, I don't have the time.

If you are embroiled in a conflict with someone who will not listen without interrupting, letters can be effective, but follow up face-to-face if possible. Anything in writing runs high risk of misinterpretation.

8. Admit your mistakes and ask forgiveness

Although we would like to think we are right and our adversary is wrong, especially if they instigated the conflict, the truth is that we create conflict together. I am not advocating that you shoulder blame when you are not responsible. But I do know that I almost always mess up somewhere in the process. Conflict is so emotionally hypercharged that only Jesus Himself can go through it error-free.

Had I confessed my prejudice to Sarah, I believe the conversation would have taken a new direction. Sarah was still at fault. She did not address her grievances directly to me but caused dissension among the other leaders. She needed to deal with her bad attitude toward the training. She needed to consider whether she lacked faith in her refusal to wait upon God's opening a teaching door. I had good reasons to be irritated, but my response was unloving and colored the entire transaction.

My role as a leader was to love her despite these imperfections and work with her to see them for herself. True, I was young and immature myself, but I cannot excuse myself on those grounds. My flaw was that I refused to lay down my rock, seeing her instead as an enemy—thus disobeying a key command that is the subject of the next chapter.

Remind people of these things and solemnly charge them before the Lord not to wrangle over words. This is of no benefit; it just brings ruin on those who listen.

—2 Timothy 2:14–15

Discussion *Questions*

1. Why is good communication so challenging, especially with an adversary?

2. Do you assume you know other people's motives without a healthy discussion, allowing you to hear from them? Why do you think this is so prevalent among women?

3. Describe a time when you jumped to a conclusion about another's motivation and then learned you were wrong. What did you learn?

4. Name ways to be kind to an adversary during the conflict resolution process.

5. What is ethos? What kind of ethos paves the way for positive peacemaking?

6. Summarize what you think it means to "lay down your rock first". What strategies will encourage your adversary to disarm and engage in a healthy resolution process?

Love Women Who Wound

Chapter 6

Therefore, as the elect of God, holy and dearly loved, clothe yourselves with a heart of mercy, kindness, humility, gentleness, and
patience, bearing with one another and forgiving one another,
if someone happens to have a complaint against anyone else.
Just as the Lord has forgiven you, so you also forgive others.
And to all these virtues add love, which is the perfect bond.
Let the peace of Christ be in control in your heart (for you were
in fact called as one body to this peace), and be thankful.

—Colossians 3:12–16

Sarah, the uninvited teacher from Chapter Five, spoke words that
still burn my ears. Near the end of our unfortunate attempt at resolving our conflict, she looked me square in the face and said, "I
don't sense that you love me." She was right. I had allowed my irritation with her to squelch my love for her. And I knew how she
felt. Remember Sylvia who tried to have me sacked over our different views on grace? During our year-long conflict, Sylvia told
a friend, "I know I'm *supposed* to love Sue." But she did not love me,
and I felt her hatred. Both Sylvia and I failed to love our enemy,
and our lack of love colored the entire process, dooming its outcome.

Loving women who wound is incredibly difficult—impossible in our own strength. But if we want to thrive in ministry
we must learn to love our enemies. And we can because Jesus
promised us that "nothing is impossible with God."[1]

Life is not easy. It can be good, but it is not easy ... We must discover God's power to care about others when our heart is breaking; we must find God's love to reach out to lost people even though our pain continues. We must learn to live well in a community of people who are sometimes wonderful, too often unspeakably evil, and usually somewhere in between.[2]

JESUS' MOST CHALLENGING COMMAND

You have heard that it was said, "An eye for an eye and a tooth for a tooth." But I say to you, do not resist the evildoer. But whoever strikes you on the right cheek, turn the other to her as well. And if someone wants to sue you and to take your tunic, give her your coat also. And if anyone forces you to go one mile, go with her two. Give to the one who asks you, and do not reject the one who wants to borrow from you.

You have heard that it was said, "Love your neighbor" and "hate your enemy." But I say to you, love your enemy and pray for those who persecute you, so that you may be like your Father in heaven, since he causes the sun to rise on the evil and the good, and sends rain on the righteous and the unrighteous. (pronouns changed by authors)

—Matthew 5:38–45

Arguably one of the toughest commands in the Bible, loving our enemy is especially difficult when we sense a woman is on a holy crusade to destroy us and God's work. Let's wring out the passage, define this kind of love, and then consider how it looks in conflict.

APPLYING THE PASSAGE

What does the passage say? Jesus taught that, when wronged, instead of retaliation we are to serve the one who wounds us and seek peace through our actions. Even if she attempts to hurt us, we don't lower ourselves to her level by striking back. Instead we surprise her with kind acts.

In New Testament times, Roman soldiers could press civilians into service—for example, they could ask Jews to carry heavy loads for them.[3] Jesus said to surprise the soldier by carrying the load twice as far as he demands. Respond unnaturally. Your enemy expects you to fight, demand your rights, and hold on to what is yours. But just as God showers both those who love him and those who don't with sunshine and rain, we treat our adversaries with love and kindness, the way we treat our friends.

Paul added to Jesus' strategy in Romans 12:19–21:

> Do not avenge yourself, dear friends, but give place to God's wrath, for it is written, "Vengeance is mine, I will repay," says the Lord. Rather, if your enemy is hungry, feed her; if she is thirsty, give her a drink; for in doing this, you will be heaping burning coals on her head. Do not be overcome by evil, but overcome evil with good.[4] (pronouns changed by authors)

The imagery of heaping burning coals on your enemy's head represents your desire to shame her into a new heart attitude. Your hope is that your kindness will cause your enemy to experience pangs of conscience that will lead to contrition and regret, an attitude more conducive to reconciliation.[5] You are changing the ethos of the argument.

The Bible asks us to consider what is preeminent. An article of my clothing or a block of my time is not nearly as important as reconciliation in a relationship, peace in the community, and God's good name. So give your coat away and go the extra mile, even though it's unfair, inconvenient, and irritating.

Jesus is not telling us to give in to our enemy's every demand, but instead to be willing to give in on issues that *are not as valuable as peace and reconciliation.* We must learn to judge between crucial and petty issues.

WHAT IS LOVE?

What kind of love is Jesus talking about in Matthew 5:38–45? In a conflict, He asks us to emulate the high and holy love of God. We can never love exactly the way God loves because we are flesh and finite, but we are called to imitate Him nevertheless. First John 4:19 reveals that "We love because he loved us first." God loved us before we exhibited any affection for Him, before we followed Him. The truth is that in our sin we are still quite unlovable—yet God loves us. His love is uninfluenced.[6] Somehow, we must learn to love our enemies the same way, uninfluenced by their disapproval, even by their meanness. We must set aside their wickedness or foolishness and love them despite the reality that they may not love us, and that they may want to do us and the ministry great harm.

Although God loves us regardless of our sin, He expresses His love to each of us differently depending on whether we are walking closely with Him or in rebellion. He does not ignore our sin. Sometimes God's love requires that He discipline us. But He always has our best interest at heart, knowing that our waywardness ultimately harms us.

What kind of loving parents would we be if we let our children do anything they pleased, such as put their hands in the fire, ride their tricycles on the freeway, or play superman on the roof of the house? The authorities would probably declare us to be unfit parents. Our love constrains us to discipline in order to insure the kind of behavior that will bring our children future happiness. And that is exactly what our loving heavenly Father does.[7]

In *God Is*, John Bisagno calls this love "a moving, powerful force that reaches out with compassion, understanding, empathy, and a desire to see that which is loved attain its full potential in life."[8]

If we love as God loves, we navigate the complex maze of knowing when to express tender love to an enemy, and when to administer a tough disinfecting kind of love. Whatever kind of love is called for, loving this way is arduous—some might say impossible—and yet it's our mandate.

AUTHENTIC LOVE DOES NOT IGNORE THE ISSUES

The people-pleaser in me finds it easy to ignore conflict and call it love, to simply end the ordeal with an easy, "I forgive you." However if I want real resolution and lasting peace, I must be willing to dig into difficult issues. Only then can honest resolution restore the relationship. Only then can I see my adversary in the grocery store and not dodge down another aisle.

Many people ignore the harm done to them and call it "forgiving" the other. In fact, one reason it may be ignored is the fear of causing conflict. When fear of the other is the undergirding motive for turning the other cheek, it cannot be called love, or forgiving the other. A lot of activity that is seen as spiritual is infused with fear, pretense, and ritual. The take-care-of-yourself movement accurately sees the potential for what appears to be loving behavior to be based on a heart that is not concerned with love, but with protecting the self or others from difficult truths.[9]

Love discerns between petty issues that should be overlooked and substantive issues that must be resolved for genuine peace to reign. If you decide an issue needs addressing, repent from fear and move into dangerous territory if you want genuine resolution and not some façade. "God's peace does not peacefully coexist with falsehood, sham, or injustice; so God's peacemakers cannot simply ignore peace-destroying sin and error, any more than a surgeon can simply close up an infected wound: an abscess is bound to develop."[10]

AUTHENTIC LOVE DOES NOT BULLY

Bulldozers can mistakenly use confrontation to unload on an adversary with unfiltered words that leave the other party assaulted and bullet-riddled. Honesty cannot excuse cruelty. American politics has become a bully pen, with different parties hiring hatchet men to demolish the character of opponents using any means necessary. Political views aside, if you keep up with politics, you often witness a cruel ethos where half-truths, innuendoes, and cheap shots are the norm. I have witnessed, and experienced this treatment myself, in the church. Christians have blasted me and others with false accusations and character assassination. Jesus must cringe. Whatever our issues, whether we are right or wrong, there is no excuse for believers to treat one another this way.

THE FOUNDATION: SELF-EXAMINATION

First we must admit our own failures to love. That's hard, but it helps to know that loving is unnatural for all of us.

I hear accounts of tragic sexual abuse, overwhelming neglect, emotional cruelty, and less tragic violations of love, which cumulatively add up to a thousand pinpricks that slowly bleed a person to death by drops. Complacency and presumption work hand-in-hand to blind even Christians to the importance of love and the inherent battle involved in learning to love. If we are to learn to love, we must begin with the acknowledgement that love is not natural and that love's failure is not easy to admit. How then does God intervene in the human personality to remove the block to love and destroy the power of evil that hates love? The answer is found in an understanding of God's relentless, intrusive, incarnate involvement and His patient forbearing forgiveness. The essence of Christianity is God's tenacious loyalty to redeem His people from the just penalty for sin.[11]

Then to love others, we must actually grasp Jesus' love for us in all our unworthiness. We must absorb His work on the cross on our behalf and plant our heart and soul in that truth. Out of that foundation will spring the love we offer others. We must take His love in as true, bask in it, and let it heal our wounds first. Only then can we enter in to a conflict with wisdom and strength, not focused on what we might lose or how we might look, but focused on loving both our enemy and our God, and seeking their good and His glory above all else.

SUCCEEDING AT THE IMPOSSIBLE

In my late twenties I (Sue) was offered the overwhelming opportunity to teach women the Bible. Although I was a ravenous Bible student and my faith was mushrooming, I had only been a believer for five years. Yet, from the first time I stood before women and saw the light of understanding sparkle in their eyes, more than anything, I wanted to teach them God's Word.

It had transformed my life and I wanted to pass on the gift. But I knew the task was impossible in my own strength. I simply did not have the resources or the ability.

But I also knew that God delights in using unlikely people. I sensed that He would enable me to do the impossible *if* I could somehow figure out how to depend on Him completely. Don't misunderstand. I did my part, but I prayed fervently every step of the process. I admitted my helplessness. I told God that I was just a little girl who needed her Father to guide her. I gave God plenty of time by working ahead.

In my heart, I was on my face before Him, pleading for help as I worked. On the day before I taught, as the process neared its end, I rested in solitude. Please don't think I am trying to impress you with my super-spirituality—I was simply desperate for help. Before I slept, as I lay my head on the pillow, I intentionally entrusted the message to God and asked Him to carry me as I taught. He did. God used *my* feeble words to change lives. His supernatural presence did the impossible. A similar heart attitude is a prerequisite to loving our enemies, requiring the same desperate surrender.

Preparing to meet with an adversary necessitates similar preparation. In some ways I find sitting across from an enemy more challenging than speaking to a room of five hundred women. At least when I teach the Bible to a large group, I can plan my message carefully. It's a one-sided conversation. In a conflict, I should think through what I want to say; I may even write out a plan, but I can't script the actual conversation. I don't know what my adversary will say or do. Moment by moment, I am dependent on the Holy Spirit to enable me to respond with love.

Jesus knew His followers would face a similar challenge. The week before He was crucified, He told them what to do when they faced an adversary.

> You will be brought before kings and governors because of my name. This will be a time for you to serve as witnesses. Therefore be resolved not to rehearse ahead of time how to make your defense. For I will give you the words along with the wisdom that none of your adversaries will be able to withstand or contradict. You will be betrayed even by parents, brothers, relatives, and friends, and they will have some of you put to death. You will be hated by everyone because of my name. Yet not a hair of your head will perish. By your endurance you will gain your lives.
>
> —Luke 21:12–19

We can trust God for the kind of power He promised the disciples. The Holy Spirit does enable us to love our enemies and respond with words that surprise us—*if* we seek His help earnestly, allowing Him to carry us. With God all things *really* are possible. However, notice in the passage that the disciples are not guaranteed a positive outcome—they may be physically murdered. The promise is that even in death God will ultimately bring them into His presence. We are not guaranteed the resolution we desire either, only the power to act rightly in the midst of the process.

DISTINGUISH BETWEEN
DIFFERENT KINDS OF ENEMIES

One valuable skill is the ability to discern between different kinds of enemies, enabling us to love each appropriately—sometimes with tender love, sometimes with tough love.

Allender and Longman in their excellent book *Bold Love* conclude with instructions on how to love people according to Solomon's categories in Proverbs:[12]

- The wise woman
- The simple woman
- The foolish woman
- The evil woman (scoffer)

Of course, each individual is unique and no one fits neatly into one of these four categories. Some women are a combination, exhibiting foolish actions in some areas and wisdom in others, even fluctuating day by day. Nevertheless, looking at common characteristics can help us love different women appropriately.

Loving a wise woman

If you and your enemy are wise women, and you both draw on your wisdom, the reconciliation process should be smooth and quick. Each of you will probably interact honestly, listen intently, attempt to understand one another, and work together toward a God-honoring conclusion. You can let your guard down with a wise woman. The ethos will still be tense, especially at first—after all, it is a conflict—but the tension should relax as each sees the other acting reasonably. The solution is likely to be straightforward. Tender love flows more naturally toward a wise woman who wants to love you back. Loving a wise enemy should not be nearly as complicated as loving simple, foolish, or evil women. These kinds of women require different expressions of love.

Loving a simple woman

Loving a simple woman is not as challenging as loving an evil woman or a fool. Allender and Longman label this sort of woman as a "normal sinner."

The biggest struggles of a normal sinner are with envy, naiveté, and poor judgment. The simpleton seems to lack the ability to see danger and make sound, wise decisions to avoid it. They seem to wander naively toward the precipice of terrible harm, but never quite choose the direction of foolishness, or, on the other hand, prudence and wisdom. Simpletons are fence-sitters, but they have an openness to rebuke and wisdom that augurs well for them, if they are warned early enough to avoid the way that seems right but then leads to destruction . . . The simple usually do not succumb to cold violation or hot anger, but instead pine after what they do not have and envy those who do.[13]

In Proverbs, Solomon paints a picture of the simple woman: "A simple woman believes anything, but a prudent woman gives thought to her steps" (14:15 NIV). "The simple inherit folly, but the prudent are crowned with knowledge" (14:18 NIV). "Flog a mocker, and the simple will learn prudence . . ." (19:25 NIV). (Feminine rewording on these and other passages have been added by the authors.)

LOVING STRATEGIES WITH SIMPLE WOMEN

How do you love a simple woman? Take time to develop an authentic relationship with her. Teach her, encourage her, believe in her, and model wisdom to her. Show her unconditional love, overlooking petty issues and concentrating on big ones. Plug her into Bible study and make sure wise women surround her.

Conflicts with simple women sometimes arise out of their envy of others, leading them to gossip and bicker. Their inexperience in ministry coupled with their pining to be noticed can lead to problems. They tend to volunteer for roles for which they have no expertise or ability (a good reason not to ask for volunteers when you need leaders). Simple women criticize leaders' decisions, completely unaware of what is involved in leading a ministry. I (Sue) experienced more conflict with simple women than with fools or evil women. Most petty skirmishes were with simple women and they could be handled quickly and successfully.

Loving a foolish woman

How do we distinguish a foolish woman from a simple one? A fool is impulsive, reckless, undisciplined, quick-tempered, and self-indulgent, yet she is often warm and caring, until you cross her. Then she blows up or melts down. A fool exhibits addictive behaviors. She doesn't think about the consequences of her actions, so she is often making messes. She likes a quick fix and lacks common sense. We all act foolishly from time to time, but that does not mean we are all fools. A fool exhibits these traits consistently and is resistant to correction.

Solomon on fools

Proverbs is pregnant with warnings about fools. Consider ways these proverbs might help if you are in conflict with a fool:

Fools mock at making amends for sin, but goodwill is found among the upright. (14:9 NIV)

A fool spurns her father's discipline, but whoever heeds correction shows prudence. (15:5 NIV)

Better to meet a bear robbed of her cubs than a fool in her folly. (17:12 NIV)

A discerning woman keeps wisdom in view, but a fool's eyes wander to the ends of the earth. (17:24 NIV)

A fool's lips bring her strife, and her mouth invites a beating. (18:6 NIV)

A fool gives full vent to her anger, but a wise woman keeps herself under control. (29:11 NIV)

Encounter with a fool

Occasionally I (Sue) accompany my husband, a lay prison chaplain, into a prison or jail. I met Leslie on a visit to a minimum security facility. Young and attractive, yet crippled, she impressed me with her quick wit and no-nonsense demeanor. Resistant to the gospel at first, she answered my probing questions about Jesus honestly and intelligently. I was drawn back into conversations with her over and over during the weekend. Saturday evening, she invited me into her private space, an upper bunk. There she told me her story.

Her parents were "religious" people and cocaine addicts. Her father was distant, her mother hysterical. In high school, she ran wild, giving birth to a son at fifteen. The boy's father was a black athlete, and Leslie admitted that she intentionally had sex with him to enrage her bigoted father. She was angry at his passivity and restrictions.

One afternoon, Leslie found her mother in a pool of blood. She had committed suicide. Leslie showed me her mother's blood-stained note, tucked away among the few possessions she brought to prison. After her mother's death, she abandoned her son to the care of her sister and pursued a life of fun, exotic dancing, drugs, and finally prostitution to support her habit.

The "life" took its toll and one night she jumped off an overpass. I wondered why she limped when she walked. She fractured her pelvis, sustaining a debilitating injury. Upon release from the hospital, she returned to the party scene, stole money for drugs, and was now serving time for possession and robbery. Was she a fool? Yes, but is she today? I don't know.

Leslie prayed to receive Jesus as her Savior on that top bunk, and we parted friends. I left her my contact information, but I never heard from her. As we analyze Leslie's responses to life we see a pattern of reckless, selfish behavior. True, this lovely woman was scarred by her mother's suicide and her father's lack of love, but her life was strewn with impulsive acts, with little regard for outcomes or the welfare of her son. Yet, she was a warm, smart woman, easy to love during those two days. But if she were my biological sister or a woman in my ministry, I would find it difficult to love her if she continued to live as a fool. You will find women like Leslie in church. What if you find yourself across the table from a woman like her in a dispute?

Loving strategies with fools

How do you love a fool? If a fool persists in foolish attitudes and actions, confront her. She is likely to respond badly, in anger or hysteria. Do not be influenced by her tirades. Love her with tough love. Expose her foolishness and silly behavior. Communicate clear consequences if she continues, and force her to face them. If you are a mother or grandmother, draw on your mothering skills—for in many ways, a fool is childlike. If she repents, be ready to offer long-term mentoring to help her learn self-control, discipline, and wisdom. Again, love her with a tough, redemptive love.

Loving an evil woman
face-to-face with evil

On my inaugural trip with my husband's prison ministry, he was sent to a maximum security men's unit near Amarillo and I was sent to the largest women's penitentiary in west Texas. It was August and none of these facilities is air-conditioned. Huge fans circulated parched air, making the prison feel like the world's largest hair dryer, with outside temperatures topping 102 degrees that weekend. I shadowed my "coach," Janice, all day, even when she insisted we visit Block C, known to house the worst troublemakers.

When Janice asked to go in, the officer, secure behind thick steel and glass, responded, "I can't let you in there. They threw an officer off the third tier a few months ago." I turned to go, but Janice persisted until I heard the loud clunk of the heavy door release. On a mission from Jesus, she boldly entered with tentative me on her heels.

When entering a prison dayroom, one looks for a friendly face. Usually many smiles greet you, inviting a visit. Most incarcerated women are not evil women. The majority have made horrific choices, with almost 60 percent former alcohol or drug addicts.[14] They can't wait to spread out pictures of their kids on the cold metal tables where they've gathered. But the evil ones glare at you or look away.

As we charged into Block C's dayroom, only one woman

smiled. Janice immediately slid onto the seat across from her and began to connect. I stood shaking, alone in a sea of scowls. But Jesus sent me for a purpose and I was determined to find out what it was—even in this hellhole. (I did not know He was providing an illustration for this book.)

Before me sat a woman who resembled an albino Jabba the Hut from Star Wars. Her hair was stark white, her eyes a piercing pale blue, and her four hundred pounds dripped sweat. When she saw my Bible, she gushed King James verses in an eerie monotone voice. Was I afraid? You bet, but at the same time, I sensed the Holy Spirit taking charge, another opportunity for desperate surrender. I sat down. After a bit of small talk, she explained that she had been wrongly convicted of several husbands' murders. Sure. Normally, inmates never tell you why they are there—another red flag.

She leaned close as if to pull me in and asked if I could help her find a better lawyer. I explained I was not there for that purpose. Then I told her about God's love and Jesus' sacrifice on her behalf. She recoiled. She eyed me strangely and then said, "You know, I could really hurt you, but there is something between you and me." I nodded and replied, "Yes, it is the Holy Spirit protecting me." She grunted and I walked away. I have looked into the eyes of evil and they cowered in the presence of the Lord.

Evil in disguise

Some people are easily labeled evil—Adolf Hitler, Charles Manson, Jezebel, and the albino convict. Evil women like her are easy to identify. If this woman is ever released, and I doubt she will be, she is unlikely to find her way to your church. However, you will see similar characteristics in women who masquerade their wickedness behind a mask of normalcy. "Normal" evil women may know the Bible and act spiritual, sometimes super-spiritual. Just like the albino, they are often itching for a fight. They will look for ways to manipulate you for their own self-interest. They usually back down if you respond with God's strength. But these "normal" evil women are not nearly as easy to spot.

There are many people, however, who do not perpetuate societal or individual barbarity to this demonic extent but who are more than simply arrogant, hard, and hurtful. All of us are capable of doing evil things, but evil people are driven by a self-interest that is so heartless, conscious, and cruel that it delights in stealing from others the lifeblood of their soul. Often the one who delights in evil is an ordinary, unassuming person who hides behind a façade of normalcy. Few people who are evil ever appear evil, even after the evidence of their deceit, destructiveness, and hardness is exposed.[15]

The mother who constantly criticizes her children, undermining their dreams for the future, ridiculing their decisions, and spoiling their relationships, may look like an overly enthusiastic parent but instead may be a malicious, jealous woman who enjoys sucking the lifeblood from her offspring. The elderly deacon who runs off multiple pastors may seem like a committed Christian leader but in reality may use his office to secure his own power, unconcerned about the damage to the pastors and their families.

Solomon's portrait of evil

In Proverbs, Solomon writes about evil women, also called "the wicked" and "the scoffer." Note how often these proverbs pertain to conflict.

The words of the wicked lie in wait for blood, but the speech of the upright rescues them. (12:6 NIV)

An evil woman is bent only on rebellion; a merciless official will be sent against her. (17:11 NIV)

Drive out the mocker, and out goes strife; quarrels and insults are ended. (22:10 NIV)

Do not fret because of evil women or be envious of the wicked, for the evil woman has no future hope, and the lamp of the wicked will be snuffed out. (24:19, 20 NIV)

Identifying an evil woman

How do you know if your enemy is evil? Underneath, an evil woman is cold-blooded, crafty, conniving, and void of emotion. She usually hides it well so you can't always know, but consider these red flags. If throughout the process, your adversary exhibits patterns of truth-twisting, agreeing to peace but doing everything possible to stir up more trouble, attempting to annihilate your reputation with falsehoods and then claiming innocence, exhibiting disregard for authority, showing no guilt or shame when exposed, and frolicking in destruction—well, your adversary may be an evil person.

Loving strategies with evil women

If so, you proceed with caution. You must garner all your strength to defeat her attempts to destroy you, your ministry, and the Lord's reputation. You must love her, but with tough love. This kind of love says, "I will not allow you to win. I will stand in your face and call you on your behavior. I won't be intimidated or manipulated. Neither will I hate you as you hate me, but instead I will love you. I will expose you with surprises, all for your good, hoping that you repent and change. If you refuse, I will still love you, but I will not allow you to wreck the ministry, destroy me, or wreak the damage you desire."

In the next chapter, we will walk you through the Matthew 18 reconciliation process. This involves several steps, each one including more people. Loving an evil woman is likely to necessitate a lengthy process. We suggest that you follow this process carefully, soliciting the help of others when allowed. It often takes a team to defeat evil, and you will need the prayers and support of colleagues. Jesus knew that evil people exist and He gave us the tools in Matthew 18 to limit their damage and perhaps restore them.

Create a loving ethos

Jesus commands us to love our enemy, whether she is wise, simple, foolish, or evil. Conflict resolution strategies differ depending on the adversary, but in every case, we treat her with kindness, dignity, and a strength that does not settle for an easy but dishonest peace. As we attempt to live out these qualities, the ethos we create in the conflict serves as an incubator for a positive outcome. Remember, ethos is the environment or climate we create as we interact with our adversary.

A place for Yvette

Yvette seemed to enjoy her studies at Dallas Theological Seminary, until her first assignment in my course came back with a low grade. She had completely disregarded the instructions. In response, my co-teacher Joye and I received a caustic email. She accused us of being unfair and prejudiced because she was black, but she did not give an example.

Joye and I met to pray and discuss our response. Because we had both been accused, we could tackle the conflict together. First, without defensiveness, we evaluated the charges. We had worked for several years on the instructions to ensure clarity, handing them out in written form. We determined her first accusation invalid. Next we tackled the complaint of prejudice. We replayed our interactions with Yvette, attempting to honestly assess whether or not she had grounds for her feelings. We were at a loss, but we needed to hear specific charges. We were sincerely open to correction.

As we thought about a meeting, our intent was to create an ethos that would lead to a positive outcome. We needed a quiet, private place on campus. The décor in my office is designed to encourage women and foster intimacy, so we decided to meet there. When Joye called Yvette, her voice was kind but firm as she explained that we cared about her and wanted to hear her out. Yvette made an appointment for the next day.

To kick off the meeting, Joye and I prayed that we could resolve this issue for everyone's benefit and that Jesus would be honored in our words and actions. Obviously nervous, Yvette did not pray aloud. Joye and I did everything we could to calm her. We circled up the chairs and offered her cold bottled water, as tension almost always makes one thirsty. A painting of Jesus cuddling a lamb hung within her view. The first thirty minutes, we gently asked her questions to learn more about her background. Although we were nervous too, we intentionally spoke with warmth.

She opened up, telling us that she moved to Dallas to attend seminary with her husband and three small children. In his fifties and disabled, her husband was still unemployed so now she was working to support the family, in addition to carrying a full course load and caring for her children. We listened intently and entered into her stressful life.

When the time seemed right, I said, "Yvette, we want to talk about the email you sent us. We want to understand more clearly why you were so upset, and to see what we did to offend you, so we can work on our failures. But we also need to tell you that blowing up at professors when you receive a low grade is unacceptable." She apologized for her outburst and admitted that she had not taken time to read the instructions before plunging into the assignment. We explained that attention to detail was required in graduate school, and that other professors would not tolerate vitriolic emails.

Next we asked her, in a warm but firm tone, to give us an example of our prejudice. She began to cry. We offered a tissue but asked again for a specific example. She could not give us one. Through her tears, she apologized again, thanking us for our honesty and care. The remainder of the time we discussed how to help her alleviate her overload and manage her stress. We offered several tangible solutions, including short-term financial aid. The session ended with a final prayer and hugs.

Yvette did not return to class and soon dropped out of seminary. I am sad, but, in her circumstances, she made a wise choice. I hope she will return when the time is right. As I review the conflict, I believe it was a success and I sense God's pleasure. Joye and I loved her with appropriate love throughout the ordeal. We were not defensive. We were willing to learn if we had erred. But neither did we back down from confronting her about her behavior. Encased in our care and kindness, she responded with contrition. Then she acted wisely.

MISSION ACCOMPLISHED

When we look back over a conflict, our goal is to know that we loved our adversary with the kind of love God offers each of us—a tender love mixed with strength. God enabled us to love Yvette and she knew it. If we can love our enemies, we have created an ethos that moves the likelihood of good outcomes much higher on the scale of possibilities. And whatever the outcome, we can look back without regret, knowing we have obeyed our Lord's command—we have loved a woman who wounded us.

If anyone says "I love God" and yet hates his fellow Christian, he is a liar, because the one who does not love his fellow Christian whom he has seen cannot love God whom he has not seen.

—1 John 4:20

Discussion *Questions*

1. What does it mean to "love your enemies" in the spirit of Matthew 5:38–45?

2. According to the Bible, what is love?

3. What is "tough love"? When is "tough love" called for in a conflict? Have you loved anyone with this kind of love? Describe the situation, the outcome, and any insight that might help the group. (No names, please).

4. Why is it impossible to love our enemies in our own strength? How then can we love them?

5. Distinguish between simple, foolish, and evil women. In your opinion, which is the easiest to love? the most difficult? Why?

6. Have you learned to love a simple woman? a fool? an evil woman? If so, how? (No names, please.)

Steps *to* Making Peace *with a Sister*

Chapter 7

If your sister sins, go and show her her fault
when the two of you are alone.
If she listens to you, you have regained your sister.
But if she does not listen, take one or two others with you,
so that at the testimony of two or three witnesses
every matter may be established.
If she refuses to listen to them, tell it to the church.
If she refuses to listen to the church, treat her
like a Gentile or a tax collector.

—Matthew 18:15–17
(pronouns changed by authors)

More than 40 percent of Australian Tasmanian devils are dead because these vicious little dogs constantly bite one another while fighting for food, spreading a rare, fatal cancer called Devil Facial Tumor Disease. Scientists found that abnormalities were identical in every tumor, indicating that the disease began in the mouth of one sick animal and spread from dog to dog as bits of the tumor broke off one dog and lodged in the facial wound of another. Over the years the tumors spread, now killing thousands of devils.[1]

Tasmanian devils are not the only species to wound their own with their mouths. As we have seen, we Christians sometimes exhibit devilish behavior toward fellow believers. Jesus knew we would need help in our disputes. His words in Matthew 18:15–17 provide a wise conflict-management process, but unfortunately this text is one of the most neglected in the Bible.

Matthew 18:15–17 contains Scripture's most direct teaching about the difficult task of resolving conflict. Jesus commands Christians to face conflict head-on, laying out steps designed to lead to reconciliation, peace, and harmony. His strategy is specific and straightforward, but we observed in Chapter Two that many women prefer an indirect posture when they disagree. We women need to pay particular attention to Jesus' words if we are serious about pleasing God and overcoming disputes His way. We need to master the skill of managing conflict and Matthew 18:15–17 shows us how.

As we dissect and commit to apply this passage, we can become skilled peacemakers, but it won't be easy. Many of us will need to work hard to unlearn negative habits and tendencies. But would you prefer to endure wounds caused by conflict like the Tasmanian devils? The end result could be equally disastrous. We dare not ignore Jesus' step-by-step instructions in Matthew 18:15–17.

OUR GOAL IN THE PROCESS

What is your goal during the Matthew 18 reconciliation process? Is it to walk away the victor? Do you want to show you are right, make your opponent look and feel foolish, or regain your "good name"? Is the reconciliation table the place to prove your point? If so, according to Stone, Patton, and Heen of the Harvard Negotiation Project, you need to work toward a different goal. They describe a better approach:

> Instead of wanting to persuade and get your way, you want to understand what has happened from the other person's point of view, explain your point of view, share and understand feelings, and work together to figure out a way to manage the problem going forward . . . Changing our stance means invit-

ing the other person into the conversation with us, to help us figure things out. If we're going to achieve our purpose, we have lots we need to learn from them and lots they need to learn from us. We need to have **a learning conversation**.[2] (emphasis ours)

Pray that God will enable you to shift your goal from thrashing your opponent to learning, connecting, and truly understanding your adversary. With that motivation in mind, let's explore Matthew 18:15–17.

Step One: Go and Show

If your sister sins, go and show her her fault when the two of you are alone. If she listens to you, you have regained your sister.

Primarily for believers

Note that there are two parties in the conflict: the offender and the offended. Both are assumed to be Christians, as indicated by the term "brother," or in our case, sister. The word for "brother" is *adelphoi*, which refers here to believers both male and female. No excuses, women. Jesus intends this process for you too!

Two things are important to remember: First, this situation refers to believers, fellow Christ-followers. While the peacemaking principles within are valuable to anyone, the steps involved may not apply easily to nonbelievers. Second, Jesus is speaking to men and women who have committed to following Him. These steps are open for any man or woman to employ with any other fellow believer.

Who takes the initiative?

Jesus instructs the offended to be the initiator in the peace process. If a woman wounds you, *you* are to go to her. What if you are not personally wounded but instead you observe an offense to God or someone else? Notice the words, "If your brother sins, go . . ." Some Bible translations include the words "sins *against you*, go . . ." but scholars believe that phrase was added by scribes in later centuries after the original gospel was penned. Why is this important? Those who read translations that include the added phrase "against you" may believe that a confrontation regarding sin must only take place when the sin is committed against oneself.

For instance, if I discovered that someone has been slandering me, this text gives me permission to go to that person for resolution. But the scriptural text does not limit discussions about sin to just interpersonal ones; believers are free to confront another's sin even if it has nothing to do with themselves. For example, you observe a church member—a self-proclaimed believer—checking into a hotel with a woman you know is not his wife. Do you say nothing because he hasn't done you, personally, wrong? No, you are free, and responsible, to ask this man to explain himself. Sin dishonors God, no matter whom the action is directed against. And the point of confronting sin, indeed the entire point of our lives, is to bring honor and glory to God. So, Jesus exhorts His followers to confront sin no matter where they see it being committed.

But notice that in either case—an offense against you or an observed offense against another—the offense is called a "sin." What constitutes a sin? Sins listed in the Bible include sexual immorality, debauchery, coarse joking, theft, drunkenness, idolatry, witchcraft, hatred, discord, jealousy, rage, anger, selfish ambition, envy, bitterness, slander, gossip, quarrelling, and pride (Galatians 5:19–21; Ephesians 4:31; 2 Corinthians 12:20). Is the offense truly a sin? Do you have concrete evidence? Are you evaluating an action you have observed or a heart attitude you suspect? The answers to these questions should affect your attitude as you go. If you are hurt but unsure whether the offense was actually a sin, you are wise to go asking questions rather than with an accusatory attitude.

Personal preferences and differences of opinion are not sins. Disagreements over methods or grey issues, including doctrine, are not sins. Personality clashes are not sins. If you assume or "feel" disrespected but have no concrete evidence, wisdom dictates that you consider carefully whether or not to proceed with a meeting to discuss the "offense." You may be right, but you will look silly confronting a sister on the basis of intuition or a "feeling." Notice that anger, hatred, rage, envy, quarrelling, and bitterness are listed in the Bible as sins. These are emotions as well as actions and attitudes. Even God feels the emotion of righteous anger at times, and of course, God does not sin. But if you feel offended and allow those feelings to fester into unrighteous anger, rage, hatred, or bitterness, then you have sinned. Going to a sister and confessing your own sin in response to her offense might be the first step at resolving the offense committed against you.

Holding on to a perceived offense can cause emotional turmoil, resulting in distance, anger, depression, even bitterness. Directly giving the "offender" an opportunity to explain her view of the situation is probably a wise choice, but enter this discussion humbly, admitting you may be wrong. Many "offenses," particularly among "intuitive" women, are merely misunderstandings and will easily be resolved with honest, direct, and tentative talking. But before you go, ask the Lord to help you discern whether or not you are truly dealing with "sin."

When should I overlook the offense?

Whether or not the offense is actually sin or a perceived misunderstanding, the Bible gives us the option of overlooking the offense. Proverbs 19:11 says, "A person's wisdom makes him slow to anger and it is his glory to overlook an offense." The Hebrew word עָבַר (*avor*) means to "pass over." The construction of the proverb shows the relationship between anger and overlooking, assuming that when one can overlook, there will be no anger.[3]

W. McKane says, "The virtue which is indicated here is more than a forgiving temper; it includes also the ability to shrug off insults and the absence of a brooding hypersensitivity . . . It contains elements of toughness and self-discipline; it is the capacity to stifle a hot, emotional rejoinder and to sleep on an insult."[4]

Again, many offenses are merely misunderstandings, miscommunications, innocent though hurtful. As we said before, these may not even qualify as sins. Each situation is unique and must be evaluated individually. Many of these offenses can be easily dismissed without hard feelings, forgiven graciously in the secret places of your own heart, no words necessary to anyone. You must decide, "Can I pass this over? Is it important enough to bring it up in conversation? Do I need an explanation or confession? Or can I let it go with no hard feelings?"

The trick here is that we must be truthful with ourselves. Let's say that my friend Stacy reveals information about me to another friend—information I specifically asked to be kept confidential. Yet it does no harm and turns out to be inconsequential. Nothing comes of it. What then? Do I scold Stacy for talking out of turn? Perhaps. A gentle reminder may be the best course to take. Or maybe the situation was so minor that it truly didn't bother me and I can let it go without resenting Stacy. I will have to decide. (Regardless, I can remember this lesson about sharing confidences with Stacy for future reference.)

Ask yourself, "Can I chalk this up to a bad day? Can I interact with my offender without this offense coloring our relationship?" If you can, forget it! But if I find myself a few days or weeks later rehashing Stacy's "betrayal" and gossip, having imaginary conversations with her about what an awful friend she turned out to be, that's a sign of underlying bitterness. If I see her in the grocery store and turn down another aisle to avoid her, that's a red flag. I haven't let it go, like I thought I had. Her actions truly did hurt and have damaged our relationship, whether she is aware of this or not. It's time to *go* to her, in the spirit of Matthew 18.

Am I in denial?

Don't confuse "overlooking" with denial. Many women would prefer to resign from their commitments rather than discuss the conflict openly with their offender. The thought of expressing the hurt face-to-face is ranked with having a root canal or giving a political speech to an audience of opponents—no one looks forward to the experience. There is the possibility of greater misunderstanding and even rejection. But with prayer and Christlike love, you may leave the meeting with a more intimate, authentic friend than before.

If you refuse to face the conflict, you'll pay a price over the years. Possible consequences include a bitter spirit that colors your outlook on life and loss of intimate friendships. We all wound one another from time to time. Refusing to become skilled at reconciliation will doom you to a lonely life of superficial relationships. And you will be ignoring a direct command of your Savior.

The principle of containment

Suppose you have determined that God would have you move ahead and confront your offender. Pay close attention to Jesus' words "when the two of you are alone" or, as the New International Version (NIV) interprets the text, "just between the two of you."

Jesus limits the first meeting to the two parties—and no one else should know about the conflict. When I am hurt, the first thing I want to do is call my closest friend or corner my spouse and unload—a huge temptation for women who rely on others for support and feedback. I may try to fool myself into believing I am doing this to gain wisdom or convince myself that I need a sounding board. Sometimes that is true, but more often, I want to give my listener the chance to agree with me. And when the conversation is over, I have given my listener the gift of carrying the offense with me.

If you really need a "sounding board," go to a professional counselor, trained to keep quiet and far more likely to give you a balanced perspective. If you can't afford a professional, find a woman who has no relationship to the situation, someone out of state who might understand and could give wise unbiased counsel. Resist the temptation to draw in women entrenched in the issue.

Disregarding Jesus' instructions by refusing to contain the conflict often births coalitions that later mushroom into factions, tearing apart communities, churches, and families. Even if the two parties meet and resolve the dispute, my initial listener, who was not privy to the peace process, may continue to carry the offense long after I and my offender have laid it down.

It is here that many women disobey Jesus and sidetrack the peace process. It is here that many conflicts escalate out of control, before the two parties have even met for resolution once. We cannot overemphasize the importance of listening to Jesus here. Sisters, ignoring Jesus' principle of containment is sin!

The birth of a coalition

Martha walked out of the meeting in a daze. She had worked for children's minister Cheryl for seven years, initially enjoying her job, but recently feeling that the routine had become drudgery. More and more she spent time at the women's shelter downtown and she could sense her passion for working with children waning. Her attitude had colored her performance. Cheryl noticed and asked Martha to let someone better suited to children's ministry take her position. Martha had realized this day was coming but the finality shook her nevertheless. What would she do for needed income? The family counted on her paycheck to make ends meet. And she would miss her coworkers and the status she enjoyed, being on staff at her church.

As she drove home, the words "I have just been fired!" swirled in her head. Anger against Cheryl simmered. But her habit was to trust the Lord and to commit situations like this to prayer. She squelched her resentment toward Cheryl and began to pray, asking for a godly response and direction as she embarked on the transitions ahead.

However, as she opened the back door, emotions escalating, she had an overwhelming desire to call Darlene. A founding member of the church and long-time friend, Darlene considered herself the unofficial "mother of the church." Although she never held a staff position, she loved to be involved in church business. Martha felt a catch in her spirit as she dialed the phone but she "needed a sounding board" and a shoulder to cry on.

Darlene exploded, furious with the children's minister. Darlene accused Cheryl of an unloving attitude, caring more about programs than people on her team, and acting independently from God. Surely a woman of prayer would never have made such a foolish decision as letting sweet Martha go. As Martha listened, a sense of righteous indignation crept up into her tensing shoulders. Her neck broke out in red blotches. Darlene slammed the phone down with, "This is not right. I'll find out what's really going on."

Like a holy crusader, Darlene sped to the church and marched into the children's ministry office, cornering Cheryl's assistant. "I just stopped by to see how you are doing," oozed Darlene. But within a half hour she was probing for information related to "changes I hear about around here."

Cheryl's assistant later reported the incident to her boss, explaining her discomfort and confusion at the conversation. Cheryl was livid. "How did Darlene know? Martha must be talking."

The next day half a dozen "influential" women in the church received a call from Darlene just to inform them of the injustice, and of course, swearing each one to secrecy. In addition, the elder board received an email from Martha contesting "an unfair firing" and asking for reinstatement and an investigation. A nasty conflict was born with long-term consequences for the children's ministry, and particularly for Cheryl and Martha. Trust annihilated, Cheryl resorted to gathering a group of her own, pitting two coalitions against one another for an ugly battle that dirtied the name of Jesus. After several months of wrangling, Martha, Darlene, and several of her friends left the church in a flurry. And Martha's husband and daughter, carrying an offense for their dear wife and mother, turned their backs on the Lord for years to come. Cheryl continued in her position as minister to children, but with reputation soiled and enthusiasm sapped, she struggled for several years to lead with the same fervor.

Characteristics and consequences of coalitions

What is a coalition? Rubin and Brown penned this definition: "The unification of the power or resources (or both) of two or more parties so that they stand a better chance of obtaining a desired outcome or of controlling others not included in the coalition."[5]

Coalitions are common and can be positive, as when several people band together to influence a decision that benefits them all. At the heart of coalitions is the desire for power—power to get what *we* want done. But coalitions can be harmful and dangerous, as seen in the previous illustration.

Christian women tend to feel powerless in a variety of situations. They are usually outnumbered on staff and in leadership roles in the church. Some are voiceless and feel powerless in their jobs and homes. As a result, they tend to come together to "feel" stronger.

Many women thrive in a web of relationships. They lead using collaboration and team-building. A woman's natural tendency in conflict is to seek to draw a supportive net around herself, first to assure herself that she is right, and second, to comfort her in the inevitable emotional "tension" over the disagreement. These female tendencies toward power-building, relational support, and collaboration make many women vulnerable to ignoring Matthew 18:17, to their peril.

Consequences range from drawing in and wounding bystanders, especially family members, to creating widespread dissension in the body of Christ to ultimately dirtying Jesus' name. This domino effect splits churches and turns nonbelievers against Jesus, coloring His reputation in the culture. If Martha had resisted her temptation to call Darlene into the conflict, the end might have looked very different. Jesus was dead serious when He taught us the principle of containment!

A positive example

I (Kelley) left my child with my friend Donna on the day I left for a ministry speaking gig. My son woke that morning not feeling well, but not overtly sick, and I felt he was not contagious, and I felt pressured to go with my plans—I had a plane to catch and no babysitter backup. A week later I called her to thank her again for her help and to share how my trip went. Her manner was oddly clipped, even cold, and I was baffled. About an hour later, she called back to explain her previous attitude. It seemed that my child's condition was more contagious than I'd thought and had forced her to cancel her day's plans with him and her own children. While I was out of town, they had come down with the same mild but irritating condition, so her offer to help turned into a week's inconvenience and building resentment. She told me that she hadn't even realized how upset she was until she heard my voice on the phone and all sorts of angry feelings arose.

Thankfully, Donna realized what was happening and decided to confront me with my offense. She did not want to let the resentment fester and affect our relationship, especially if I was clueless that she had such feelings. And while I was mortified and completely embarrassed at what I'd inadvertently done to her, I was also glad she was honest enough to tell me, forgive me, and make peace between us again. Something seemingly minor could have poisoned our friendship.

What did Donna do right? She obeyed Jesus' command to "go and show." She saw her responsibility as the "offended party" and did not leave me in the dark, trying to figure out her coldness, for long. She resisted the temptation to talk over the situation with mutual friends first. She was direct and kind but did not hide her emotions. As a result, through honesty and forgiveness, a breach in our relationship was avoided, and we continue to enjoy the sweet gift of companionship as we share our journeys as mothers of young children. This was Jesus' desire when He spoke Matthew 18:15–17. How might our lives and world be different if we determined to "go and show, just between the two of you"?

Step Two: Take Witnesses
But if she does not listen, take one or two others with you,
so that at the testimony of two or three witnesses every matter may
be established.

Jesus says that if the first meeting is unfruitful, the offended party is responsible to call a second meeting and invite witnesses. In this verse, Jesus quotes Deuteronomy 19:15. According to

Mosaic Law, when an accusation was made, witnesses were to tell any related truth. A witness is there to testify to the truth or false-hood of the offender's account. But suppose there were no wit-nesses to the offense? What value are third parties if they have no evidence to present?

Witnesses serve several functions, regardless of whether they can shed light on the facts or not. Jesus is asking those who may have insight concerning the offense to join the parties and help sort out relevant details. Third parties provide evaluation during a discussion that affects the conflicting women. Their nonverbal feedback, such as facial expressions and body language, are pow-erful influencers. If third parties are allowed to comment from time to time, they may serve to settle the ethos and move the dis-cussion toward rational conclusions. They may see solutions that neither party has considered.

> The mere presence of an audience (including psychological presence) motivates bargainers to seek positive, and avoid neg-ative, evaluation—especially when the audience is important to the bargainers. The external audience helps keep the bar-gaining process honest. The effect of the negotiator's behavior before a watching world provides a check-and-balance system so that grave injustices are less likely to occur.[6]

Gangel refers to the influence of a formal negotiator in this quote but the affect is the same with any respected third party. I am astounded at how differently Christian women view an event they both witnessed or a conversation they both heard. Third par-ties often help the two parties see the conflict honestly.

How to choose "witnesses"

If a third party actually observed the offense, then he or she is obviously the "witness." But more often a third party has not witnessed the offense but is called into the conversation to calm the tone and bring needed balance and insight.

The offended party is still responsible for initiating this second meeting and overseeing the decisions and processes involving witnesses. But how can the offended party carry out this second step in a manner that contributes to the peace process rather than inhibits it? First, the offended party should see this as an opportunity for fairness. If the other party believes you are "stacking the deck" by calling in third parties who will take your side, then you have set the stage for trouble—and again a breach of trust.

Who will you call as the third party? If possible, collaborate with the other party on this decision. Ask the other party for names or give them a say on your choices. Can you bring someone you both respect? Should you include a leader who has some connection to the offense? For example, if the offense took place in a Bible study, should you call the Bible study leaders? Yes, if you feel they can be neutral in their assessments.

What should you do if you cannot agree? Consider each asking someone to serve as third parties, but ask the other party to bring someone who will not simply be their advocate. We suggest not bringing family members who may struggle to be impartial. The goal is to bring in people who can help both of you with blind spots and possible solutions neither of you may have considered.

Step Three: Take It to the Church

If she refuses to listen to them, tell it to the church. If she refuses to listen to the church, treat her like a Gentile or a tax collector.

If Jesus' instructions have been followed, there should be no more than four or five people aware of the conflict. They have met together, hoping for reconciliation, forgiveness, and peace, but alas, none has been found. What now? Jesus says to take it to the church. What in the world does that mean?

Two hardworking, respected women were unable to settle their dispute in the church at Philippi, and Paul placed the issue squarely in the laps of the leadership. In Philippians 4:2–3, Paul writes, "I appeal to Euodia and to Syntyche to agree in the Lord. Yes, I also say to you, true companion, help them. They have struggled together in the gospel ministry along with me and Clement and my other coworkers, whose names are written in the book of life."

Women, whoever God has placed in authority over you in the church is now in charge. This might be a staff member, deacons, or elders. Often women in conflict find themselves presenting their case to male leaders. Sometimes gender differences hinder an effective peace process at this point. Chapter Nine will guide male leaders entrusted with helping women in conflict. We have seen too many men treat a female conflict the way they would a disagreement between two brothers, with negative outcomes.

Again, courtesy dictates that all parties are heard at the same time. The two women may meet with all the elders or selected representatives. They may simply sit down with their senior pastor or a counselor he has recruited. The process is now in the hands of the leadership and the role of the two parties is to submit to it. Certainly, each party can and should express their perspectives if they believe the process needs tweaking, but bottom line, what the leadership says, goes.

In the conflict where Sylvia attempted to have me thrown out as a false teacher, the executive pastor ultimately served as overseer of this third step. He was wise and fair. After the first session, he looked both of us square in the face and bellowed, "I don't want either of you to say one more word about this to anyone. It is settled." He breathed the fire of fear into me and I respected and obeyed his mandate. I did not say a word to my team or any other women in the church. But my opponent continued to slander me at every opportunity. In the end, I was exonerated. Neither of us handled the conflict perfectly. But God worked to protect my reputation and open significant future doors for me—and His favor was, I believe, partly because I listened and followed my leaders.

Whether our spiritual leaders are right or wrong, they are God's chosen, and we owe them respect and obedience, unless they are clearly going against Scripture. Godly people follow the directions of their leaders. Then we can rest in the assurance that the outcome will ultimately be God's best for us. If we cannot follow our leaders, the other choice is to quietly and respectfully find leaders we can follow, without defaming the ministry.

Leaders are not perfect and often make mistakes. But when the mantle of ministry is on their shoulders, they are God's anointed, and God frowns on those who treat them with contempt or disrespect. Certainly, we are free to give them constructive feedback and they should be accountable to others, but we must trust that God is working in their lives to refine them as better leaders.

Does Matthew 18:15–17 include church discipline?

Actually, all the steps mentioned previously fall under the umbrella of "church discipline." But often in the American church we give that designation to the final, church-wide disciplinary sanctions toward an unrepentant believer. When this sort of church discipline is contemplated, we must consider its purpose and the manner in which it is dealt.

Why is church discipline necessary?

We sometimes think of church discipline as punishment, but it is not—it is discipline, designed to train and restore, much as a loving, authoritative parent acts toward a wayward child. Scripture commands it, as Matthew 18:15–17 attests. Other Scriptures affirm the premise that discipline demonstrates love—the Lord disciplines His children (Hebrews 12:6) just as earthly parents discipline their children (Hebrews 12:9–10). We liken it to "tough love." We make things uncomfortable for the offender to encourage repentance and restoration.

Scripture describes several instances of church discipline. Second Thessalonians 3:6, 14–15 says,

> But we command you, brothers and sisters, in the name of our Lord Jesus Christ, to keep away from any brother who lives an undisciplined   life and not according to the tradition they received from us . . . But if anyone does not obey our message through this letter, take note of him and do not associate closely with him, so that he may be ashamed. Yet do not regard him as an enemy, but admonish him as a brother.

The church in Corinth allowed sexual sin to flourish before Paul admonished the leaders to take action.

> . . . now I am writing to you not to associate with anyone who calls himself a Christian who is sexually immoral, or greedy, or an idolater, or verbally abusive, or a drunkard, or a swindler. Do not even eat with such a person. For what do I have to do with judging those outside? Are you not to judge those inside? But God will judge those outside. *Remove the evil person from among you* (1 Corinthians 5:11–13, emphasis ours).

Another crucial reason for church discipline involves our witness to the world. Allowing blatant sin to remain unchecked, an unrepentant sister to continue in full fellowship with the local church, dilutes and dishonors the holiness of God. First Peter 1:16 reminds the church that God says "you shall be holy, because I am holy." Allowing ungodly behavior to continue within the body sends a confusing message to the world, which is watching and judging us.

Finally, church discipline supports the harmony and unity of the church body. It says that the whole shall not be disrupted, distracted, or deceived by an individual bent on an ungodly course of behavior. In his response to the Corinthian situation, Paul writes, "Don't you know that a little yeast affects the whole batch of dough? Clean out the old yeast so that you may be a new batch of dough" (1 Corinthians 5:6–7).

Practical implications

Jesus says to treat the unrepentant believer as a Gentile or tax collector. Gentiles were not given full privileges in the temple or synagogue. Tax collectors were considered traitors to their people, since they collected taxes for the Romans, often pocketing a surplus for themselves. Neither group was accepted into the mainstream of Jewish life in Jesus' time. In similar fashion, according to Matthew 18:17, unrepentant sinners should not enjoy the privilege of being a trusted and intimate part of the Christian community.

Denominations and other churches vary in their methods of exercising discipline. Generally, there is a gradual increase of severity, from admonitions to warnings, followed by rebukes both private and eventually public. The final step is called excommunication, or removing that person from membership rolls and barring her from voting privileges, the communion table, access to sacraments and church assets.

Our manner

However, this is not your opportunity to humiliate, degrade or beat down your sister. Nor is it your opportunity to retaliate or let loose your fury at being hurt. Jesus admonished us to "love our enemies," and we are called to pray for her, asking God for her good and for her to come to her senses and return to full fellowship. Your hope is for complete restoration and peace. Your social interaction may change but your heart attitude of love does not. Should she repent and return, trust has probably eroded and will need to be earned back—but love remains.

While disciplinary actions may seem and feel harsh, we must monitor our own motives during the process. Be sure that anger, desire for control, vengeance, or self-promotion do not drive the engine of discipline forward. Our manner toward the one at fault must be righteous, propelled by a desire to protect Christ's reputation and grief at sin's dominance in that person's life.

THE PURPOSE OF THE PROCESS

What blessings can we experience as we learn the skill and art of peacemaking with other women? Through conflict, we can see God at work in issues and relationships; we can learn more about His character and faithfulness as well as more about ourselves.

Conflict resolution can mature and equip us. It can prepare us to minister in the real world. Although we often tend to view conflict negatively, Jesus said, "Blessed are the peacemakers, for they will be called the children of God" (Matthew 5:9).

If possible, so far as it depends on you, live peaceably with all people.

—Romans 12:18

Discussion *Questions*

1. Why is Matthew 18:15–17 particularly difficult for women to apply? Does that mean women can ignore the passage?

2. What should be our goal as we embark on the Matthew 18 process?

3. How do we decide whether or not to overlook an offense?

4. How difficult is the "principle of containment" for you? Can you recall a time when someone attempted to draw you into their conflict? How did you respond? (No names, please.)

5. Why are coalitions so dangerous? How do they get started?

6. Who can be a "witness" in a dispute? How can "witnesses" be helpful?

7. In your opinion, why do Christians often ignore Matthew 18:15–17?

Prepare Your Team *for* Women Who Wound

{ Chapter 8

I am not praying only on their behalf, but also on behalf of those who believe in me through their testimony, that they will all be one, just as you, Father, are in me and I am in you. I pray that they will be in us, so that the world will believe that you sent me. The glory you gave to me I have given to them, that they may be one just as we are one—I in them and you in me—that they may be completely one, so that the world will know that you sent me, and you have loved them just as you have loved me.

—John 17:20–23

A GOOD PROBLEM

Kristi dreamed of creating a ministry to mothers of boys. Growing up with sisters, Kristi initially felt overwhelmed and unprepared to parent her four boys, now ages six to twelve. But with the help of mentors and a shelf of resources, she was learning—and she felt the Lord leading her to gather other mothers of boys to learn from current material, seasoned experts, and one another.

Her church contributed an ample budget and space. The Lord provided seven women who shared her dream and were willing to commit to lead the ministry with her. They planned, prayed, and played together. They were friends and coworkers, united around a common goal. If they disagreed, they worked hard toward consensus, leaving final decisions to Kristi, their trusted and competent leader.

Within two years more than a hundred mothers of boys from her church and the surrounding community met monthly for instruction, inspiration, and prayer. In small groups, they gathered around tables for conversation and encouragement. The fellowship hall provided a perfect meeting place until the third year. That year, a larger than expected registration forced Kristi and her team to look for a bigger room, except such a room did not exist at their church.

The team met to discuss what to do. They looked at options. Move to another church or a recreation center? Ginger pushed hard for the ministry to relocate to her sister's church on the other side of town. But when Kristi met to discuss the issue with her church's senior pastor, he insisted they stay put. Kristi's ministry served as an entry point into the church, and the new member class was bulging. His solution to the facilities problem? Simply replace the round tables with rows of chairs. The room could hold up to double the participants if they ditched the round tables.

Kristi felt a catch in her spirit. How would stadium-style seating affect the intimacy they worked so hard to build in the small groups? But she felt pressured to comply as no alternatives emerged and the first gathering was two weeks away. When she met to tell her team, they agreed it was the best solution under the circumstances and adjourned, eagerly anticipating another exciting year.

"BUBBLE, BUBBLE, TOIL AND TROUBLE"

The year began with a bang, with mothers bringing friends and speakers bringing helpful instruction. But by November the team noticed a slight slip in attendance and by January the dip was evident to everyone. The team wondered why. They did not voice their concerns, not wanting to appear negative or disloyal, but the leaders grieved silently as they saw their numbers wane.

Kristi missed the team's January prayer meeting. A church in another state had heard of their ministry and asked her to help them start a similar ministry in their church. Ginger voiced her "concern" in the form of a prayer request. "Kristi has taken on so

much this year. She's got her family to care for and now she's off
helping other churches start up ministries like ours. I'm just wondering how much time she has for prayer. I just don't want her to
burn out. I think we should all take it upon ourselves to pray for
her daily—for her priorities and her prayer life."

The request was dripping with sweetness. The other women
on the team had not noticed that Kristi was so busy. Was she overcommitted? Was she sacrificing her family for the ministry? Was
it wise to travel to other churches when her own priorities might
be misplaced? Seeds of dissension had been planted. Over the
spring, Ginger continued to needle team members with "concerns" about Kristi, mostly one-on-one and always couched in sugary caring. But as the team wrestled with lower participation, it
was easy to blame Kristi. *She must not be praying enough. She must
be too busy. God can't honor her leadership. Now He has pulled His blessing from the ministry.*

Was Kristi overcommitted? Maybe so, but maybe not. Even if
she was, Ginger's behind-the-back tactics are not God's way. Harriet realized Ginger's actions were sinful and her motivation probably suspect. Finally, after another call from Ginger to discuss
Kristi, Harriet picked up the phone to inform Kristi, who, of
course, was irritated and felt betrayed. Now Kristi viewed Ginger
not only as her personal enemy but also as an enemy of the ministry she worked so hard to plant and sacrificed to maintain. Kristi
should have confronted Ginger immediately, giving Ginger an opportunity to explain and repent. But she did not. A conflict en-
sued that ultimately hurt the ministry and divided the team.

DRAGONS, DRAGONS, EVERYWHERE?

No, there are not dragons, dragons, everywhere. But it only
takes one. Never assume that an unhealthy woman like Ginger
isn't hiding on your team, looking just like the other women. She
may be ambitious, jealous, or simply believe that you should lead
the ministry differently, like she would. Many of us could be a
"dragon" to someone else, given a certain scenario. Teams are
composed of people and people are sinners, under the influence of

their "flesh" as we observed in Chapter Two.

A TIME OF PARTICULAR VULNERABILITY

Be aware that your team is still susceptible to conflict even if the ministry is thriving and the team is working in harmony. Kristi had her hands full leading the ministry and probably did not see the need to train her team to manage conflict effectively and biblically. After all, they were working well together. But, in time, conflict will rear its ugly head in the best of ministries. And thriving ministries today can easily become struggling ministries tomorrow. Ministry success vacillates. Although Kristi's decision to reconfigure the seating was forced upon her, the negative consequences to the small groups harmed the ministry, causing discouraged leaders. Watch for dragons to emerge in a downturn!

Discontented women look silly complaining or planting seeds of doubt about a leader when things are going well. But when problems or challenges arise, an unhealthy woman often takes advantage of this fertile ground for gossip and dissension. Be on guard.

PREPARE AHEAD CAREFULLY

What could Kristi have done differently to prepare her team for inevitable conflict? When is the right time to equip your women for disputes? The right time is now. A wise leader understands that Satan *loves* to use conflict to destroy ministry. He will blindside you, finding the tiniest crack in your armor, or your team's armor, and wiggle his way through. One heated and badly handled conflict can take you down. Few other issues can inflict this kind of damage. Training leaders to be skilled peacemakers is foundational and top priority.

How to Equip Your Team
Understand what's at stake

Healthy teams are composed of people who trust their teammates and their leaders. They know that their leaders won't tolerate one team member bad-mouthing another. This confidence breeds trust, creating a place where women can dream big, work passionately together, and be real with each other. Healthy teams are founded on trust. Trust births honesty, creativity, and the freedom to be one's self.

How is trust undermined? It happens all the time. Suppose I am upset about my teammate's comments during our last gathering. But instead of talking directly to my teammate about the incident, I decide to talk to my leader, behind my teammate's back. My leader listens empathetically and attempts to help me process the issue. Her desire is to help me "work through" the conflict. She thinks she is acting as a peacemaker but in reality both of us are gossiping.

Is this really gossip? Ask yourself, would my teammate be upset if she knew I was talking about her to my leader? Of course! Would I be upset if she did that to me? Again, of course. This "secret" meeting is unhealthy for me, for my leader, and for the whole team.

Now my leader and I have a "secret" about my teammate. I can't be sure what my leader is thinking. She may be irritated and worried that I'm a troublemaker. How will this conflict play out on the team over time? Or I may have planted critical thoughts about my teammate that my leader did not see before. Now she is battling a critical spirit too. And *nothing* has been done to resolve the differences. Now both of us carry the conflict and it colors all three relationships.

In the process, my leader has learned something important about me. I am not to be trusted. I am a gossip. And if I gossip about my teammate, I am just as likely to gossip about her one day when I disagree with something she does as my leader.

I have also caused my leader to gossip—which, by the way, is sin. My leader might defend herself by arguing, "I was only listening. I was being a sounding board for my friend." But gossip is not only talking about someone behind their back. It is also listening. It takes two to gossip, and both the one who talks and the one who listens are equally guilty.

What do you do if a woman on your team comes to you

complaining about a teammate? The instant you realize what she is doing, stop her and insist that she go to the woman involved. And you follow up the next day to be sure that she has. You make it clear that on your team no one is allowed to process conflict unbiblically. We will not accept anything outside of Matthew 18:15–17. Understanding this reality builds confidence that each team member will be treated fairly and that no one can bad-mouth another without their knowing it.

This strategy also forces women who disagree to either overlook the conflict or talk about it openly to one another. Openness allows for understanding, forgiveness, and reconciliation. The slate is clean again and teammates can move forward, working together to accomplish their shared goals. If they continue to spar, the Matthew 18 process kicks in, resulting in ultimate reconciliation or possibly one woman leaving the team. Either way, trust remains intact. The team can continue their work for the Lord.

Refusing to follow Jesus' instructions means death to a healthy team. It's like unleashing the Ebola virus. It's hard to kill, easy to catch, and it leads to slow death. Understand what is at stake and go to extreme measures to root out anything that threatens trust on your team.[1]

Require a "peacemaking" covenant

A covenant is a formal, solemn written agreement or promise between two parties relating to the performance of some action. When members of your team sign a peacemaking or conflict resolution covenant, they are promising to manage conflict according to set guidelines and principles. I asked my team to re-sign this covenant yearly, as a review. For new recruits, the pledge served to inform and instruct them on how our team managed conflict.

Create a covenant that works for your team. An example is provided on the next page that you may adopt or tweak.

Conflict Resolution Covenant

As a member of the (your organization name), I agree to follow the biblical pattern for resolving conflict in Matthew 18:15–17.

If your sister sins against you, go and show her her fault, just between the two of you. If she listens to you, you have won your sister over. But if she will not listen, take one or two others along, so that 'every matter may be established by the testimony of two or three witnesses.' If she still refuses to listen to them, tell it to the church; and if she refuses to listen even to the church, treat her as you would a pagan or a tax collector.

This means:

1. If I am offended and cannot overlook the offense (Proverbs 17:9, 19:11), I will contain the conflict by "going and showing her the fault, just between the two of us." If I need counsel, I will consult a counselor or ministry leader. I agree not to involve other parties as this can lead to factions. (2 Corinthians 12:20, Proverbs 16:28, James 4:11a)

2. If the conflict is not resolved after I "go and show," I will work to resolve the conflict with a third party. (You may want to list yourself or another ministry leader here if you want to be involved in conflicts that relate to your own ministry.) I agree to involve only "witnesses" who might help resolve the differences in a gracious and godly manner. I agree not to discuss this matter with those who are not directly involved.

3. If the conflict is still not resolved, I can "tell it to the church." However, I will not go to "the church" without informing my ministry leader (You may want to list yourself here as well.) as well as the other party. If I meet with "the church," I agree to invite the other party and my leader to go with me so that we can all be heard at the same time.

Name _____

Date _____

Signing a covenant is helpful and emphasizes the seriousness of the issue. However, signing a document is no guarantee that an unhealthy woman on your team will honor it. Dragons are experts at excusing their foolish or unethical behavior, even if they have signed a pledge saying they won't act that way. In addition, team members may sign the covenant without really understanding what it means. As their leader, your responsibility is to teach them what the covenant entails and to give them opportunities to practice.

Provide quality instruction

Effective leaders are constantly building into their teams. Pepper your gatherings with instruction, case studies, and discussions about pertinent topics. Share the teaching with team members who exhibit ability as teachers and trainers. Include conflict resolution training in your regular team retreats. Certainly it merits a place in your leadership development program with other important topics like team-building, communication skills, or small group leading techniques.

Block out enough time to adequately teach on this important topic, possibly six to eight sessions. Consider using this book as core curriculum for a series of lessons, especially because you are working with women, who process conflict differently than most men. Ask the team to read a chapter and then discuss the questions at the end or use the stories as case study discussions before reading the chapters as a teaser. For additional general resources, contact Peacemaker Ministries (www.hispeace.org).

As you wrestle with conflict issues and case studies, watch how your team members interact and be alert for unhealthy patterns that may signal potential dragons. Spotting an unhealthy woman early gives you time to ward off problems, or, worst case, to replace her. Also remember that unhealthy patterns are sometimes the result of ignorance, and excellent training may extinguish dragon-like qualities. What a blessing for the woman, the ministry, and the Lord!

Model peacemaking skills

Peacemaking is like teaching the Bible, baking a pie, or playing a musical instrument. You can know a lot about these aptitudes but still lack proficiency when asked to actually *do* them. As a result, signing a covenant, studying a book, and discussing case studies are not enough. Peacemakers must practice peacemaking. But like so many skills, it helps to watch a master. Leaders should strive to become master peacemakers if they expect their team to hone their conflict resolution abilities.

A master peacemaker does not fear conflict but sees it as an opportunity for growth and understanding. She lives out peacemaking skills in her personal life, with family, friends, and co-workers. Matthew 18:15–17 is second nature to her, applied consistently without thinking. For example, when a woman in her ministry makes an appointment to complain about a team member, the master peacemaker stops the conversation immediately with the question, "Have you talked to _____ about this offense before bringing it to me?" And if not, which is often the case, she insists that the Matthew 18 pattern be followed.

When a master peacemaker is offended, she prepares herself emotionally, prayerfully, and quickly. Then she sits down with the "opponent" to clear the air and work toward harmony. If she senses a dispute between team members, she encourages them to do the same and follows up when needed. If she hears gossip clothed in a prayer request, she confronts the offense kindly but firmly, nipping this sin in the bud. If she observes a clear offense to another, she is willing to allow her name to be used in the peace process—none of "Oh, I heard Sally gossip, but don't ever tell her it was me who told you." Refusing to stand up and be part of the process shows a lack of courage and hinders true peacemaking. Model your willingness to risk a relationship for the sake of honest peace.

A master peacemaker has control over her emotional responses so that she is not overwhelmed by criticism. She is able to think clearly in the midst of the dissension, without her identity threatened.

Becoming a master peacemaker takes years of practice, but a serious leader sets this goal, knowing that she cannot expect others to develop peacemaking skills if she does not become proficient herself. The task is more difficult for some women than others, particularly for extreme people-pleasers and bulldozers. But the future health and often survival of the ministry depends on our perseverance.

Again, create the right ethos

As you, the leader, become more and more skilled at peacemaking, and you effectively train your team, you will create an ethos where peacemaking is the norm. It is expected and thrives. Women who struggle with unhealthy conflict patterns, women who are prone to gossip, and women who like dissension are more likely to look for more lucrative territory elsewhere or they will change.

Years ago, a woman in my church called me to ask my view on repentance. She reported that she had just come from a home Bible study where another woman defamed me by insisting that I did not believe repentance was necessary for salvation. I had never taught that nor do I believe it. I was extremely grateful that this woman called to clear up the matter instead of accepting it and I wondered how many other women left assuming this falsehood about me was true.

I thanked the woman and informed her that what she had heard was slander. Gossip is inappropriately repeating a matter but slander is repeating a matter that is false. I asked her to tell me the name of the slanderer but she refused, claiming she did not know. I doubt that, but this response is typical in this kind of situation. She did not want to be identified to the hostess either. Many women refuse to allow their name to be used, hindering the biblical process. However, she did give me the name and phone number of the hostess. How should I proceed?

I knew I needed to confront the offender but I did not know who she was. After praying and working to calm my emotions, I picked up the phone and called the hostess. I informed her that I was aware of the situation and would very much like to talk with the offender. The hostess was obviously shocked and after considerable stammering and sputtering, she consented to call the slanderer and ask for a meeting. I informed the hostess that I would call back the next day.

When I called back, the hostess told me that the slanderer would not identify herself but she was sorry for her erroneous comments and she would not make them again. The hostess also apologized profusely and I thanked them both—after a respectful short lesson on Matthew 18, which I asked the hostess to pass on to the anonymous slanderer. I have found that a direct, bold, but kind approach will over time create an ethos, a trickle-down effect that ultimately squashes unhealthy conflict.

Team members will discuss their differences respectfully, kindly, directly, and without overreacting. They will learn to focus on the issue they disagree on, not broadening the dispute to the personal. If they are offended, they will know how to proceed privately, following the steps Jesus taught them.

Yes, what we have described is the ideal, and you won't ever "arrive" because women will continue to struggle to overcome the discomfort and fear that naturally accompanies conflict. But you can create an ethos that lessens unhealthy conflict and encourages healthy patterns. When you do, you cut down on destructive conflict and you know what to do if it erupts.

When should leaders intervene?

Shannon modeled expert leading skills in her small group, one of many in our women's Bible study. Her group was off to a solid start—until Audrey cornered Shannon after the study to complain.

"I'm allergic to toxins in perfume, deodorant, hair spray—stuff like that. Today I noticed I'm stuffing up because of these odors. Could you ask the group to refrain from using these products when they come to Bible study? I'm afraid I'm going to have to drop out of the group otherwise."

"Well, I don't know. That's a lot to ask. Do you have any

medicine to help counteract the allergy?" asked Shannon, suddenly self-conscious about her twice-daily spritz of *Beautiful.*

"Well, yes, but those medicines make me feel like an airhead.
Besides, those toxins aren't good for anyone. I have to breathe pol-
luted air whenever I go out. At least the church should provide
clean air," rebutted Audrey.

"That's ridiculous!" Shannon huffed. "I can't ask the women
not to use deodorant or hair spray just because you are oversensitive to the smell . . . "

According to Matthew 18:15–17, Jesus first asks Shannon and
Audrey to attempt to work out their differences "just between the
two" of them. That's the optimum solution. However, when
perfume-happy Shannon and allergic Audrey began discussing the
issue, the tension only escalated, ending in a stalemate. And this
situation is more complex because it involves ten other women—
their small group members. They have come together to study
God's Word, and the group's emotional and spiritual growth is
potentially in jeopardy due to this conflict.

Also, leader Shannon is accountable to the Bible study coor-
dinator, the minister to women, and ultimately the male leadership
of the church. When should leaders involve themselves in a conflict with far-reaching consequences for the people they shepherd?
No formula exists, but this kind of situation is different from one
that affects only the two women involved.

When I was the minister to women in my church, I asked
Bible study leaders to inform me of potential out-of-control conflicts as soon as possible. If they were not able to make peace
quickly, I wanted to be informed and to be included as a "witness"
or advisor. I felt a responsibility to the other women in the group,
as well as, to those I reported to.

Leaders do not violate Matthew 18 when they intervene in a
dispute that could damage their ministry. However, they should
strive to be fair, wise, and neutral as they interact with the parties
involved, helping them to make peace for the good of all. And
again, only those directly involved should know about the dispute.
In the argument between Shannon and Audrey, we sat down and

worked out a solution together. Shannon refrained from wearing perfume during class time and she informed the women in the group of Audrey's allergies, asking for sensitivity. As leaders, we felt this was a reasonable response. We were kind to Audrey, but firm in our conviction that insisting women refrain from deodorant and hair spray was unacceptable. Regrettably, Audrey did not agree and ultimately left the study, but we believed we handled the conflict sensibly and kindly. The group thrived and Shannon learned valuable lessons to help her when the next conflict arises.

Additional Tips for Preparing Your Team
Who's in Charge?

Sometimes a dispute involves a power struggle. The one with the most power determines how ministry will be done. Power can be either constructive or destructive. If our motivation is to use power for God's glory and the expanding of His kingdom, power is constructive. But if we wield power to bloat our reputation or to ensure that our needs are met, then we are motivated by selfish ambition. That's negative destructive power. Unfortunately, women with emotional and spiritual problems usually grasp for power for the wrong reasons.

As a leader, you want power to be in the hands of women with positive motivation, women you select and who answer to your authority and the authority over you. You want the women who serve on your team actually to be the women who call the shots. You want your organizational chart to reflect what really goes on in the ministry.

But in the real world of ministry there are two kinds of power structures—formal and informal. The formal power structure is reflected on your organizational chart, composed of women who hold positions of leadership, oversee a particular aspect of ministry, and probably serve for a limited time. These women were prayed over, are accountable to leadership, and have been invited to serve. In healthy ministries, these women are the real leaders. These women represent the formal power structure.

In contrast, informal power structures are composed of women who don't appear on any chart nor have they been asked to lead. But these women wield power nevertheless. Maybe one controls the purse strings or is married to an influential male leader. Maybe another founded the church eons ago and won't let anyone forget it. This is "her" church. We call her part of the "old guard." Some in the "old guard" believe it is their duty to guard "the way it was" and oppose anything that smacks of change.

Maybe she is the "go-to" woman—everybody knows her name. Sometimes that reputation is based on her wisdom and authentic spirituality. Sometimes it is based on fear—fear that ruffling her feathers means trouble—and most people prefer to avoid trouble.

The problem is that most church members imagine themselves as basically "nice," willing to bend to keep the peace. This gives lots of leverage, sometimes complete control, to those hard-nosed people willing to make a public scene. The group usually gives them extra space, which translates in power—power to veto programs, to overrule pastors, to alter the direction of the church. Churches can thus be victimized by people who see being "right" as more important than being "nice."[2]

The "go-to" woman's term never expires and she isn't privy to the leader's discussions, but her disapproval can kill the leader's plans. She wields informal power.

Your task as leader is to create an ethos where the informal power structure does not override the decisions and direction of the formal power structure. I'm not advocating a disrespectful attitude toward women with informal influence, especially wise women who deserve their reputations as "go-to" women, but you don't want them running the ministry. Why? "Dragons thrive when the church's formal authority and informal power structure don't match. Whenever the church office holders, elected or appointed, are different from the unofficial but widely recognized power brokers in the congregation, dragons seem to multiply."[3]

When the informal power structure has deep roots, your task is usually daunting and takes time. When women who wield informal destructive power understand that you are attempting to decrease their influence, they probably won't like you. In fact, they may do all they can to oust you or make you miserable. You are wise to respond with quiet strength and integrity, refusing to take personal affront or let their tactics discourage you. I have found that over time, as you persist and provide quality ministry, your positive power and that of your recognized team will usually increase and theirs will decrease.

Former women students write to me asking for direction and encouragement in situations where the informal power structure is strong and erecting roadblock after roadblock. In the majority of cases, the formal power structure eventually takes its rightful place, especially if the male leadership supports you wholeheartedly and expresses that support. A few times, the dragons refused to budge and my students gave up in frustration but were better equipped for their next position. While there are no guarantees that the formal power structure will always end up in its proper leadership position, abandoning the field to the dragon seldom works either.

Invest relationally in your team

Leaders are busy women, sometimes more task-oriented than relational. These focused leaders can fall prey to a blind spot. Caught up in their lengthy to-do list, they can forget to build intimate relationships with their team. Investing relationally in your team provides a plethora of benefits. It's fun to share ministry with friends. Different perspectives enrich end results. And don't forget the old adage, "Many hands make light work." It's true.

But here is another important reason: when destructive conflict erupts, you need a team for support. As appropriate, you need a team as a sounding board. You need a team to help you maintain the health of the ministry. You need a team to walk beside you and pray with you. But the team won't be there for you unless they know you well. They need to know your heart, dreams, flaws, and strengths. They need to trust you, and they won't if you have not invested in personal and deep connections. "Those who make absolutes out of issues others see as negotiable can stymie the will of the majority. Unless the church has an unusually effective board, this usually means the pastor has to fight the battle or else abandon the field to the dragon."[4]

If the relationships between you and your team are strong, you will weather storms together. If you and your team are tight, they are unlikely to fall away when the waters rise. Solomon writes:

> Two people are better than one, because they can reap more benefits from their labor. For if they fall, one will lift up her companion, but pity the person who falls down and has no one to help her up. Furthermore, if two lie down together, they can keep each other warm, but can one person keep warm by herself? Although an assailant may overpower one person, two can withstand her. Moreover, a three-strand cord is not quickly broken.[5]

Solomon was right.

I (Kelley) used to lead a small church's women's ministry. A year after I was hired, some women openly questioned my position as director of the ministry. While they had every right to express their opinions, I was out of town on that occasion and hence unable to speak up for myself. I only learned of it when a friend on my leadership team called to warn me, without naming names. She felt protective of me and thought I should at least be alerted to the situation.

The caring tone of her voice was like aloe cream on a sunburn, soothing the sharp edges of pain. I do not enjoy direct confrontation, and I knew I would have her support when the time came to deal with the situation. When the pastor later revealed the names of the dissenters in order that I might pursue reconciliation with them, I was hurt. They were regular participants in the women's ministry, friendly acquaintances who would have been among the last people—I thought—to attack me or the women's ministry.

While they repeatedly asserted that their arguments "weren't personal"—and some of their points were very objective—it felt personal. But thanks to the team member who called me, and others present who rose to my defense, I felt confident both in my position and in the work I produced for the church. I knew I was not alone. These dear friends gathered around to defend and carry me through subsequent disagreements and conversations with the dissenters. They believed in the women's ministry, and in my leadership. With their unwavering support I never felt as if my position or ministry were truly threatened. Together we formed a many-stranded cord that was not quickly broken.

Invest in your team relationally as part of an intentional plan to equip your team thoroughly, and you'll reap a variety of benefits, including shelter from women who wound.

Peace I leave with you; my peace I give to you; I do not give it to you as the world does.

—John 14:27

Discussion *Questions*

1. Why is it important to train a team to be skilled at conflict resolution?

2. How can gossip and slander damage a healthy team?

3. What should a team leader do if a team member complains to her about a teammate? Why?

4. Why should a team leader become an expert peacemaker?

5. What kind of team atmosphere produces trust, creativity, and productivity? How does a leader create this ethos?

6. Why should a team leader invest relationally in her team?

7. Picture a healthy team in your mind. What do you see? What strategic steps did the team leader employ to create this dynamic team?

The Male Minister's Guide

⎱ Chapter 9

to Female Negotiation

> So then, my brothers and sisters, dear friends whom I long to see, my joy and my crown, stand in the Lord in this way, my dear friends! I appeal to Euodia and Syntyche to agree in the Lord. Yes, I say also to you, true companion, help them. They have struggled together in the gospel ministry along with me and Clement and my other coworkers, whose names are in the book of life.
>
> —Philippians 4:1–3

WOMEN'S CONFLICT IN THE EARLY CHURCH

Two women were bickering in Philippi—women Paul knew personally. They had "struggled together [with Paul] in the gospel ministry." They were insiders, respected friends, true believers, and he cared enough to be grieved by their conflict and address the situation in his letter. What divided them? We don't know. But we know that the issue was serious, probably a threat to the unity of the church. News of the dispute traveled all the way to Rome, where Paul was under house arrest. In verse two, Paul appealed to the male leaders to negotiate their conflict, to help these women "agree in the Lord."

WOMEN'S CONFLICT IN CHURCH TODAY

Just like in Paul's day, male leaders today often find they are called to help women make peace. If you are a male leader, people in your ministry will cause conflict, and some of them will be female. When women in your ministry spar, you should care. And because you are sometimes called into the middle of these disputes, you are wise to prepare. An undisclosed part of your job description is the task of intercessor, peacemaker, and negotiator for women.

In our experience, male ministers tend to handle conflict without taking into account the gender of the parties involved. Big mistake. Men and women process conflict differently. Of course, Matthew 18:15–17 applies to both men and women. But ignoring the gender factor as you attempt to negotiate differences can severely hamper your effectiveness and lessen the likelihood of a positive outcome.

Do you understand basic differences in the way men and women process conflict? If not, your effectiveness will be compromised. You will be expecting women in conflict to act like men, and when they don't, you will be surprised and frustrated. In this chapter, we enumerate some of these differences, hoping that this knowledge will make you more skilled at female negotiation. The result will enable you to sidestep all kinds of turmoil and heartache.

IGNORE AT YOUR OWN PERIL

Bill felt more like a boxing referee than a church elder as he sat between two women who glared at each other like debating Democrats and Republicans. Rival Bible teachers Dottie and Maria were embroiled in a six-month conflict that began when newcomer Maria founded a class that welcomed women who did not reject speaking in tongues. Hard-liner Dottie did not believe anyone embracing this belief was a "real" Christian, and made her views clear to her students. As a result of her stern countenance and tendency toward legalism, about half her students dropped out of her class each semester.

In contrast, Maria held tight to the church's doctrinal statement but was quick to allow varied views on "grey" areas. Maria's numbers grew steadily each year. But as her warmth and expertise began to draw women from Dottie's classes, hostility simmered. When Maria taught a study on the book of Acts, arguing for the reality of miracles today, Dottie exploded and embarked on a campaign to expose Maria as a false teacher. Unfortunately, Maria responded by alerting her team, "circling the wagons," and gossiping.

When elder Bill and senior pastor Dwight first heard murmurings of the conflict from their wives, they discounted its seriousness and hoped it would simply go away. Their calendars were packed with important new initiatives and exciting opportunities to partner with area churches. Surely these women could work out their silly differences on their own. However, Dottie hounded them for months. As she clamored and carried on, demanding that they "discipline" Maria, they realized their "ostrich" strategy was not working. And when elder Rick informed them that his wife was so distraught over the situation that she wanted to leave the church, they took action.

Specifically, what could they do to lessen the likelihood of irreconcilable differences, factions, even a church split? What actions are wise? How does a male minister handle catfights? Consider the following strategies as you negotiate between angry hurting women.

Strategies to Help Men Negotiate Between Women

Before we go further, let's be clear: statements about the way women or men process conflict won't be true for everyone of that gender. Don't stereotype. Statements that insist that all women are one way and all men are another are false. We can say that women or men tend toward a particular attitude or behavior, but exceptions abound. For example, we could say that men are taller than women, but the truth is that some women are taller than some men. Averages don't give us reliable information about individuals. Generalities help, but not everyone fits the mold. Consider this information as you work with individual women.

Also, in this chapter, we have condensed portions of this book for you, knowing that some male leaders may not read the whole book. It is primarily written to women. However, if you find your-self in the role of negotiator for women on a regular basis, you may want to read the entire book after you read this chapter. We have included chapter links to guide you to particular topics.

It's personal

In Chapter Two, we observed that research studies back up differences in the ways the sexes respond to conflict. For example, boys on the playground fought about twenty times more than girls, but they often became good friends with these adversaries after the disputes. Girls experienced less conflict, but when they fought, they did not become friends later. Bad feelings ran deep and lasted a long time.

We observe the same patterns in ministry. Without interven-tion, often women's disputes can quickly escalate and become per-sonal. I (Sue) remember sitting in a meeting with a husband and wife who were attempting to defame my reputation and destroy my ministry. He opened the discussion with the words, "Sue, this is not personal." I remember thinking, "Not personal? Of course, it's personal!" However, he was able to compartmentalize the con-flict, to narrow it down to the disagreement.

For him, if we could resolve the issue, the dispute would be over, and we could be friends. But for me, simply resolving the issue would not heal my wounds. I was deeply hurt that a fellow Christian would say and do the things this couple said and did. From my perspective, and probably from his wife's perspective, the conflict was no longer simply about the issue we disagreed over. It had bled out into every area of our relationship.

Now we were enemies. I was cut to the core. They threatened my ministry for Jesus. They damaged our relationship in ways that would not be easy to mend. Unless we committed to work-ing through our emotions and deep woundedness, it might never be over for me. Men may see these feminine responses as imma-ture and silly, but they are typical, even in women who are spiri-tually and emotionally mature. Seasoned women still wrestle with their flesh, especially when their emotions are in high gear.

Note the example of the women in Philippi. These women were respected workers and possibly leaders. But they struggled to resolve their disputes, probably because they felt the breach so deeply. The personal nature of women's conflicts makes the dispute more challenging to resolve than most men's conflicts. The personal nature of women's disputes requires special strategies when you are called to help them make peace.

Give them time . . . lots of time

Yes, you are busy and loathe hearing details. You want to get this thing over and done with so you can get back to the important topics on your agenda. But if you really want to help these women, and you really want to avert a serious conflict in your ministry, you are going to have to bite the bullet and give them time . . . lots of time. And when you are dealing with particularly sensitive women, it will take even longer.

Consider the nature of the dispute. If they are arguing over a date on the calendar, and this is their first disagreement, then resolution may come quickly. However, if tension between them is long-standing, involving a series of offenses, then your job will be more challenging. And if these two women's relationship has deteriorated to the point that they no longer like or trust one another, your work is doubly difficult and will probably take longer still.

The longer the dispute has festered, the more time is needed for healing. In the scenario toward the beginning of the chapter, Bill and Dwight let the conflict go on for almost six months without addressing it. Emotions were raw. Unfortunately, these women drew other women into the issue. When factions have formed, male leaders must handle multiple levels of offended females. Can you think of anything worse? This reality may be a good incentive not to ignore the problem until it spirals out of control. Waiting and hoping a conflict will resolve itself is like standing on the top of a mountain on a windy day, releasing the contents of a torn feather pillow, and somehow expecting to gather up the feathers without much effort. It's not going to happen!

Giving women time means blocking out an hour, maybe

several, on your calendar or simply not scheduling another meeting afterward. Expect that you may have to meet over a period of
weeks or months. You may have to employ a counselor if the damage is severe.

I (Sue) once walked into a meeting where two women were
expected to work through their conflict. The pastor had set aside
fifteen minutes. After giving the women five minutes each to give
their side of the story and "air" their issues, he lectured for a few
minutes and then told them that the issue was over, that he did not
want to hear any more about it again. But he did hear about it
again, and again, and again. Because the issue was never really resolved, problems continued to pop up for months. Women gos-
siped. Families left the church. Leaders resigned. Ministries
imploded. A few walked away from Jesus, never to return. The
women should have obeyed their leader and stopped. But when
emotions run deep, often sin abounds. If you really want peace,
give women time.

Because men can segregate the conflict from other issues, reconciliation usually comes quicker. Men usually can duke it out and
then go out to lunch as if nothing ever happened. You won't find
this pattern with women. For women, the issue is layered, and unless you address the layers, it is not over. Women may need
space—they may not be ready to let go after just one session. The
process may require stages—a time to listen and talk, and a time
at home to consider what they heard and to decide how to respond. You may be talking about this issue two, three, or maybe
four times. The slow rate of progress may make you crazy, but if
you show your frustration, the women will know. They may try to
hurry past important milestones that short-circuit true reconciliation. So slow down and give women time and space so that you
won't have to revisit the conflict in the future.

Pray

Most Christian women want to please God. Capitalize on
their emotional bond with Jesus to counter the emotions that may
have overcome them in the conflict. Pray for these women—in

their presence. Your words may help them regain their equilibrium and perspective. An intercessory prayer may help convince them of your commitment to their well-being. Commit to, and follow through with, praying regularly throughout the process.

Listen First, Fix Later

Many times, to resolve a dispute between women, a man must start by being quiet. He should listen first, and long. Asking questions may help the women talk out their point of view, their "take" on the issue. And while they are seeking a solution from you, they may come across it themselves. Usually when a conflict has reached your office, it is tangled and complex, which requires more than a directive from you that will "fix" the problem. So be prepared to listen and ask questions.

You will need to speak into the situation in time. But initially these women need to get the issue out on the table. They need to talk about the facts of the dispute and how each interprets those facts. They need to see through the other's lenses and to understand how each one hurt the other. If you jump in with advice too soon, you will bypass a critical step of the process and hinder real reconciliation.

Take time to get to know the women involved, especially if they are strangers. Can you hear insecurities in their dialogue? What do you know about their background that plays into the issue? Can you discern their emotional state? How deep is the dispute? Watch body language and tone of voice. Listening can help you gauge where you need to take the process. Listen for negative attitudes or victim mentalities and confront them. Each woman is different and brings her own unique baggage to the table. Keen listening skills will help you create an effective strategy for this particular situation.

Stone, Patton, and Heen of the Harvard Negotiation Project argue that there are three difficult conversations we must decode in conflict: the "what happened?" conversation, the feelings conversation, and the identity conversation. Skilled negotiators hear and navigate through all three realms[1] and work to shift the process from a confrontation to a "learning conversation."[2] (See Chapter Seven for more detail on the process.)

Allow women to process their emotions

If you are married, does this sound like advice you have heard to work through conflict in your marriage? Counselors and communicators proclaim the importance of giving wives opportunity to process their emotions. Yes, the same principles apply for women's disputes in the church. Consider the double benefit of becoming a skilled peacemaker with women in ministry—you'll be more skilled at home too!

Consider identity issues

When some women are criticized, their identity is threatened. The weaker their self-image, the more likely they are to exaggerate the criticism in their own minds. As a result, they may take the criticism to heart and see themselves differently. They wonder how the conflict will affect their future. They wonder if they lack the ability to serve the Lord ever again. You may observe hypersensitivity, fear, and even depression, uncharacteristic of this woman before. This kind of negative thinking impedes a woman from healthy interaction in the reconciliation process.

If you observe imbalance and extremes in a woman's behavior, demeanor, and body language, help her understand that she may be experiencing an identity crisis. Teach her that we all make mistakes and have much to learn. Show her that the Bible helps us ground our identity in Christ—the only One who will never disappoint us. She must learn to perform for an audience of One. (See Chapter Three to help a people-pleaser or a bulldozer.)

Teach women to be more direct in their communication

The tendency of some women to be indirect in communication hinders them from working through conflict effectively (see Chapter Two). If you observe this communication style either in the negotiations or in behavior that caused the conflict, point out this tendency and the problems this causes. Challenge them to be direct, but do so with a gentle spirit and kind words unless you sense a hard heart and rebellious spirit. Then a firm, strong disciplinary style is appropriate and sometimes required. This is especially true if you sense that one or both are emotionally and spiritually unhealthy. Marshall Shelley refers to these people as "dragons" in his excellent book *Well-Intentioned Dragons: Ministering to Problem People in the Church.*[3] If you are working with a dragon, you may want to read this book, but remember it is written from a male perspective and will not always apply when you are overseeing a negotiation with women.

Teach women to stop avoiding conflict

Many women are master "avoiders." They see conflict as a threat to relationships, which are precious commodities in most women's lives. Help them understand how avoiding conflict leads to serious consequences that actually endanger relationships instead of preserve them.

Steve Roese, executive pastor of Irving Bible Church in Texas, recommends that male leaders teach women to face conflict head-on. "Try it. You'll like it," he told me. When I rebutted that most women will never "like" conflict, he agreed, and then changed his advice to, "Try it. You'll like the results."[4] Help women stop avoiding conflict so they can enjoy the multiple bene-fits this approach provides.

Teach women that Matthew 18:15–17 applies to them too

If these women are operating out of their emotions and making decisions from their "gut" instead of biblical principles, they need you to teach them Jesus' instructions. Go back to the basics with them. If, after listening to both sides process through the issue, you see sinful patterns of gossip, avoidance, slander, and the like, point them to Matthew 18. Teach them the "pure milk of the Word" even if you think they should already know it. Help them understand that you are not taking sides, nor making an emotional or calculated decision for one or the other, but that you are committed to biblical standards. And you expect them to do the same. Help them see that their particular controversy is not the exception and that sidestepping Matthew 18:15–17 is sin. (See Chapter Seven regarding the Matthew 18 process.)

Stay on point

Wounded women tend to wander wherever their emotions take them. Be ruthless in bringing them back to the facts of the issue. Answer the questions first: What happened? What are the facts that everyone can agree on? What is beyond dispute, uncolored by different perspectives?

Once the facts are clear, give each woman all the time she needs to tell her side of the story and how she was affected by the situation. Don't allow the other woman to interrupt. Then give the other woman the same opportunity. Challenge each one to listen without creating responses in her head. Let each one jot down questions as they listen.

Finally, let each one ask the other clarifying questions. Set ground rules that forbid name-calling or threats. Guide the women to mutual empathy and understanding. Ask them to summarize what they are hearing or do so yourself.

Don't allow the conversation to wander but continually remind the women to stay focused on the issue and their responses to it. Seek common ground and discern if or when they can resolve their differences. If another meeting is needed, put it on the calendar. Consider requiring the women to read this book to help them work through their differences.

Monitor possible prejudices

A recent Yale University research project discovered that men who get angry at work may well be admired for it but women who show anger in the workplace are liable to be seen as "out of control" and incompetent. The researcher recruited random men and women to watch videos of job interviews and then to rate the applicant's status and assign them a salary.

In the video, the candidates described feeling either angry or sad. Participants conferred the most status on the men who exhibited anger, the second most on the women who were sad, slightly less on the men who said they were sad, and least of all, by a sizable margin, on the women who said they were angry. The average salary assigned to the angry men was almost $38,000 compared to only $23,500 for the angry women.

In a second video, the job applicant described his or her current occupation as either a trainee or a senior executive. The participants were especially critical of the angry female CEO and rated her much lower than any of the other applicants, even the angry female trainee. Angry female CEOs were labeled as significantly more "out of control" than the angry male CEOs. This affected salaries. Unemotional women were assigned on average $55,384 compared to $32,902 for the angry women. Male executive candidates were assigned more than trainees, regardless of anger, with an average of $73,643.

The study was presented at the annual meeting of the Academy of Management, a research and teaching organization with nearly seventeen thousand members. They found similar attitudes toward anger among men and women at that meeting. Victoria Brescoll, who led the study, commented, "It's an attitude that is not conscious. People are hardly aware of it." She concludes that these findings reveal a difficult paradox "for professional women—while anger can serve as a powerful tool to achieve status at work, women may have to behave calmly in order to be seen as rational."[4]

What does this research have to do with male ministers and female negotiation? Men who harbor these kinds of unconscious prejudices against emotional women may struggle to treat them with kind respect when they display anger, sadness, or other intense emotions in the conflict. These hidden prejudgments may undermine the process and hinder a positive outcome.

Include a trusted woman if appropriate

Sometimes women can hear what men cannot, especially when other women are involved. If you struggle to grasp the intricacies of the situation, consider asking a woman on staff or a female counselor to join you. However, she must be the *right* woman. She must be neutral, above reproach, and able to keep a confidence. One advantage of bringing women on staff is that they serve as capable partners in the peace process with women.

Exclude spouses if possible

Spouses are usually aware of the dispute, and they should be. They comfort us and help us talk through our feelings. But their attendance at the peacemaking table is not a good idea. Most spouses find it almost impossible to remain neutral and their very presence adds an extra level of tension in the room.

I once attended a meeting with the elders and two feuding women where a husband insisted on sitting by his wife's side. As needed facts were presented related to his wife's actions, his face grew redder and redder. Finally he exploded in anger, clenching his fists as if he were going to hit one of the elders. His wife finally put her hand on his knee and asked him to calm down. If spouses are not directly involved in the situation, do not needlessly complicate your job by including those who will naturally take sides.

Spouses' relationships to the conflict is a complex thorny issue. In a sense they carry the offense just like those actually involved. But they are foolish to attempt to enter into the peace process. Jesus did not include them in Matthew 18.

Are you a bulldozer?

Forceful, in-your-face male leaders can scare women so much that the peace process is shackled. I interviewed an executive pastor who acknowledged that his abrupt strength caused women to shy away from him. He apologized to one woman but she later told him she was still uncomfortable around him. "That's the way he is," she surmised and felt guarded in his presence. A harsh, loud demeanor backfires when you work with women. We are not saying you should be timid in your approach but a gentler tone of voice is usually more productive with women. This pastor committed to toning down his brash attitude when interacting with women, with good results.

When is it over?

How do you know when true reconciliation has been achieved? Your goal is to help each woman understand and empathize with her opponent. Do they both see things through the other's eyes? If so, you are making progress. Do they each realize how the other feels and have they both honestly asked for forgiveness? Do you need to hammer out a practical plan together that will pave the way to lasting peace and put the issue to rest?

A quick "I'm sorry" without a real grasp of what has actually transpired will not accomplish true peace. Don't settle for surface interaction that fails to reflect insight and healing. If you do, the issue will pop up again and again and you'll be back at the table for another round.

With women, it is often hard to tell if they have *really* buried the hatchet. Follow-up questions offered a few weeks or months later may be helpful to ensure that the issue is not bubbling to the surface again, about to erupt. Is the conflict over? Are they moving on? Have they stopped talking about it? Have they laid down their rock? The women will probably appreciate that you cared enough to check up on the status of the issue.

You may find that they may have tried, but animosity still lurks. The reality is that these women may never trust one another or enjoy a close friendship. Severe disputes sometimes result in one of the women choosing another ministry or leaving the church. You can't force them to work together or enjoy one another's company. Of course, we hope that mutual trust can be restored, but sometimes we have to settle for second best, containing the conflict and working through the process.

Your reward

Just as Paul instructed the male leaders in Philippi to intervene in the women's dispute in their church, God may use you to help women in your ministry make peace. We don't know the outcome in Philippi. Neither are you guaranteed favorable results. But experience has shown us that when male leaders involve themselves in the process, women listen. Most Christian women highly respect the men who serve God in their church, especially when these men show that they value women as sisters and appreciate their contributions. You can make the difference!

There is another advantage. Have you heard the old adage, "When mama ain't happy, ain't nobody happy"? We laugh, but we know it's true. This principle applies in ministry too. In our experience, when women feel valued and appreciated, they are far less contentious. When they are neglected—left without a female shepherd to teach and mentor them, overlooked when resources are doled out, and ignored when they contribute an idea or opinion—they tend to cause more problems.

If you take the time to learn to skillfully manage female conflicts, women in your ministry will thank you. If you work with them patiently, showing that their emotional and spiritual wellbeing is important to you, most women will reward you with loyal support and enduring service for Jesus.

And you will create an ethos where peace is more likely to prevail. Ken Sande, president of Peacemaker Ministries, writes that 25 percent of the churches in one survey reported conflict in the previous five years that was serious enough to have a lasting influence on the congregation, and that 23 percent of all current pastors have been fired or forced to resign in the past.[6] Surely women were involved in some, if not many, of these disputes. Become a skilled peacemaker for women, lessen your odds, and glorify God in the process.

Brothers and sisters, if a person is discovered in some sin, you who are spiritual restore such a person in a spirit of gentleness. Pay close attention to yourselves, so that you are not tempted too.

—Galatians 6:1–2

When rumors surface. . .

Suppose you hear whispers that several women in your ministry are upset with one another but none had had the courage to talk openly. Now other women are talking about the conflict and taking sides. What should you do? We suggest you call everyone involved into the same room and confront the parties involved as well as those who are gossiping about them. Sit down and ask everyone to "come clean." Attempt to untangle assumptions and distortions. Rebuke the gossipers—and, in this instance, if you are a bulldozer, let 'er rip! The goal is to squelch the rumors and seek reconciliation.

Pastors' Wives and Women Who Wound

As the senior pastor's wife, I felt like I was living in an ocean, being pulled farther and farther out to sea. I desperately needed a life preserver because I was going under and no one was there to help me. My husband was exhausted when he came home, too tired to minister to me, and I could not trust the women in the church. I learned the hard way that many of them befriended me to use me, hoping I would take up their cause.

—A pastor's wife with
25 years ministry experience

JOAN'S STORY

Joan eagerly accepted Marcy's invitation to lunch. Joan was struggling in her new role as the senior pastor's wife, trying to discover what was expected of her. For the first six months of their new pastorate, she was busy unpacking and organizing their home while caring for her two- and four-year-olds. Nevertheless, she sincerely desired to be an asset to her husband but she was unsure how.

Marcy's husband chaired the elder board and she seemed friendly and helpful. Joan looked forward to their lunch all week, hoping to make a good friend. But she left lunch fighting tears. Marcy began the conversation by asking Joan's forgiveness. Marcy explained that she had expectations of Joan that Joan had not met, and Marcy had harbored a judgmental spirit toward her. Marcy was sorry. Flabbergasted, perplexed, and wounded, Joan wrestled with how to respond. Should she extend forgiveness? Should she ask Marcy to explain her expectations? Should she defend herself, attempting to make Marcy understand that she was doing her best to adjust to a new town, church, and role? None of these responses seemed appropriate. She filled the awkwardness with small talk and exited as soon as possible.

Joan reached out to several women over the next year. However, after these attempts turned into "fishing expeditions" for the inside scoop at the church, she wearied of finding a true friend among the women at church. Books and long phone calls with family and old friends would have to fill the void.

She attended as many women's events as her other responsibilities allowed. However, when competing Bible study leaders ferociously recruited her for their study, she realized that she could not attend both and would offend one teacher either way. She decided not to attend either class. Gradually she withdrew from the life of the church into loneliness. Her departure wounded women in the church who now perceived her as standoffish and conceited.

SURVIVAL TIPS FOR PASTOR'S WIVES

Senior pastor's wives are particularly vulnerable to women who wound, especially in churches where the pastor is expected to do and be everything to everyone. In churches of all sizes, these expectations often carry over, facilitating impossible expectations, burnout, and wounded pastors' wives.

Although senior pastors' wives often experience more personal attacks and conflicts than wives of support staff, both are likely to deal with more conflict than the average woman in the congregation. And pastors' wives from every size and kind of ministry should expect conflict as a normal part of ministry life. Some conflicts will be aimed at the pastor, some at his wife, and occasionally the attack will be leveled toward the pastor through his wife.

How can you, a pastor's wife, survive and even thrive in ministry?

- First, you must become skilled at healthy confrontation and peacemaking. Possibly more than any other women, you need this book. Read and digest it. Refuse to be intimidated by people who want to manipulate or use you to further their agenda. Just like your husband, you will need to develop the skin of a rhinoceros but maintain the heart of a child.

- Second, learn to be comfortable in your own skin. Know your gifts, and develop and use them, just like any other member of the body. You are not superwoman simply because you are the pastor's wife. Refuse to allow others to set your priorities.

- Communicate with your husband concerning his expectations. Ask him to help you weather the skirmishes and conflicts with dignity and skill. You and your husband are partners in this ministry but you are not a co-pastor, unless you, your husband, and your congregation want you to be. Together work out how much detail you want to know concerning conflicts he experiences.

- Don't hide. Women of the church need your support and encouragement. Attend the events you can, and give up trying to please everyone.

- Take your time to find people you can trust and develop relationships with them. Distance yourself from those who would wound and use you, but remain gracious and kind. Don't give them fodder for gossip. Good friends will emerge, although you will always have to guard your words carefully. Your deepest struggles and secrets may best be expressed to a confidante from another church or state.

- Seek out other pastors' wives. Attend gatherings to learn more about your unique role and for support. For example, Dallas Theological Seminary sponsors a retreat for pastors' wives every year.[7] Dr. Lois Evans, wife of Oak Cliff Bible Fellowship's Tony Evans, has created the *First Lady Conference* where hundreds of senior pastors' wives from all over the nation flock to Dallas to learn, grow, worship, and network. Find resources to inspire and equip you. Collaborate with other pastors' wives who walk in your shoes.

God has given you a gift—a powerful position of influence. But the downside is that you will experience more than your share of women who wound. Face this reality. Know what to do when you are personally attacked or must block for your husband. Despite the inevitable dragons and disputes, embrace your opportunity to make a special influence for Jesus, and you will find joy along the way.

There have been times that often I have retreated from the real spiritual battle because I was too wounded by friendly fire.

—Jeanne Ballard, pastor's wife

Discussion *Questions*

1. Describe an effective male negotiator in women's disputes. Contrast him with an ineffective negotiator.

2. Generally, how do men approach conflict differently from women? How might these differences cause confusion for both?

3. Why does a man's tendency to fix problems cause problems in a female dispute? What should he do instead?

4. How do identity issues affect women in conflict? How can a male minister help?

5. How can a trusted woman on staff help in the process? Why is it best to exclude spouses in the negotiation?

6. Why should every male minister strive to become a skilled negotiator for women in conflict?

Epilogue
To God be the Glory

Work to see that the city where I sent you as exiles enjoys
peace and prosperity. Pray to the LORD for it.
For as it prospers you will prosper.

—Jeremiah 29:7

A SACRED MANTRA

In 1935, an African American debate team from Wiley College in
Marshall, Texas, beat the white national champions, debunking
the myth that blacks are not as intelligent as whites, inspiring
blacks throughout America. In the film *The Great Debaters* their
brilliant coach Melvin B. Tolson, played by Denzel Washington,
shaped a small group of unsure students into eloquent word war-
riors.

In the film, Coach Tolson stands the group in a pasture and
drills them over and over on their mantra:

"Who is my judge?"
"God is my judge."
"Who is my opponent?"
"I have no opponent."
"Why is no one your opponent?"
"He is merely a dissenting voice to the truth I speak."[1]

Conflict with other women is not a formal debate although it
may feel like one at times. The point is not to win but to reconcile
our differences and make peace. However, we can draw vital principles from the Wiley students' sacred formula. In the midst of

conflict, remember that God alone is your judge. He knows the motivations of your heart and every action, whether it is meritorious or reprehensible, whether it follows the patterns Jesus proclaimed in Matthew 18 or not.

During the conflict I described in the opening pages of this book, several women slandered me for almost a year. I was the women's ministry director in a large prominent church at that time. The male leaders instructed everyone involved to stop talking, and I did, even leaving my leadership team in the dark. They heard rumors and gossip, resulting in awkward confusion. What were they to think? Their leader was defamed yet she remained silent. Finally, near the end of the year, the pastors pulled everyone, including my lead team, together in the same room to explain the situation and attempt to squelch the talking once more. I was granted freedom to tell them about the ordeal, and did so privately through my tears. My team responded with tender encouragement and prayer.

During that year of silence I walked the halls of a church full of whispers—about me. I feared that my reputation would be so damaged that I would never be allowed to minister for Jesus again. I remember praying, asking God to at least let me continue ministry in a small place, but please not to remove me from serving Him altogether.

What carried me through was the reality that God alone was my judge and that He knew every detail. I believed that if I held my head high, obeyed my leaders, and attempted to do the right thing every step of the way, He would exonerate me. Once near the end, in what I now describe as a crisis of faith, I melted into a depression, ready to quit. During the lengthy ordeal, God and the male leaders provided a counselor, Julie, who sat through every meeting with me and knew all about it. When I was ready to give up, she came to my home. I was curled up on the couch in my pajamas, unable to stop sobbing. She listened, loved me with kind words, and challenged me to persevere. I'm grateful I did. I have enjoyed many years of productive ministry—far beyond what I could ever ask or think. He wiped the slate clean. He restored my name and gave me precious places to serve Him.

LOOKING BACK

In the midst of a conflict that turns as ugly as this one, we are tempted to believe that the damage is beyond repair. But take heart; God can repair anything. As I emerged on the other side of the conflict and reflected back, I learned valuable lessons. I learned that God *is* faithful. I made mistakes during the ordeal but overall I continued to seek Him. I tried to do the right thing as He guided me. I learned that He really is all-powerful and He really does take care of His own.

I also learned beneficial lessons about myself. I found that I cared too much about what people thought—but this experience whipped the people-pleasing right out of me. I learned that I am stronger than I realized. At first, I was not sure I could survive, but I did, through His strength and mercy. The experience prepared me for future challenges, ministry that God knew was ahead.

TAKE HEART

Whatever you are facing, hold your head high, do the next thing right, and trust your Father. He will carry you, teaching you lessons you will need for the future. Remember to perform for an audience of One, that He alone is your judge. Speak the truth in love. When you do, you will find you don't have opponents—only other women that God loves too, who also need to learn lessons. You are not responsible for their learning, only your own. You cannot convince them to make peace. You can only do your part—that is your calling as you interact with women who wound.

A PASSAGE TO CLING TO—PHILIPPIANS 4:1–9

Paul planted the church in Philippi and felt a special closeness to the men and women there. As he concluded his letter to them, he addressed a conflict between two women.

So then, my brothers and sisters, dear friends whom I long to
see, my joy and crown, stand in the Lord in this way, my dear
friends! I appeal to Euodia and to Syntyche to agree in the
Lord. Yes, I say also to you, true companion, help them. They
have struggled together in the gospel ministry along with me
and Clement and my other coworkers, whose names are in the
book of life.

—Philippians 4:1–3

Two females were bickering—women Paul knew personally.
They had "struggled together" with Paul and others to proclaim
Jesus' message. They may have been leaders, prominent women in
the church. Whoever they were, Paul had heard about the conflict
and cared enough about the situation to recruit male leaders to
help them make peace.

Following Paul's request to the male leaders to help these
women, Paul writes several well-known passages—verses often
committed to memory. We believe that although these passages
merit broad application, they are especially helpful when we are in
the midst of conflict. That was our experience, and after all, that
is the context.

Joy in conflict

Rejoice in the Lord always. Again I say rejoice! Let everyone
see your gentleness. The Lord is near!

—Philippians 4:4–5

Happiness and joy are different. Happiness is contingent on
what happens. You won't be happy in the midst of conflict, and
God doesn't expect you to be. In contrast, joy is a deep steady assurance that, despite the circumstances, God is in control and can
ultimately use them for good. Picture rocky waves off the Pacific
coast. On the surface, you are tossed about by their fierce strength,
an unpleasant experience. But fifty feet below the raging tempest,
the water is calm and quiet. In the middle of a conflict, you often
feel tossed about, unsure of where the conflict is leading and how

it will be resolved. But even in the midst of the turmoil, you can have joy. You can go down to the sure and steady conviction that God is near and working.

Your responsibility is to trust Him in the storm, and to "let everyone see your gentleness." Yes, when your emotions are in high gear, gentleness seems unrealistic. But God does not require something He does not provide. Ask Him and He will calm you. Throughout this book, we have shown you ways to respond gently, and when your adversary sees your gentleness, she is more likely to calm down too, giving way to a productive encounter and resolution.

When your knees knock, kneel on them
> Do not be anxious about anything. Instead, in every situation, through prayer and petition with thanksgiving, tell your requests to God. And the peace of God that surpasses all understanding will guard your hearts and minds in Christ Jesus.
> —Philippians 4:6–7

It's hard to pray under fire, but it's your most powerful tool in conflict. Anxiety, worry, fear—all natural emotions in a conflict—decrease when you pray. Talk to God about every detail. Shout out how you feel if it helps. You can't shock Him. Ask Him to help you love your adversary and fill you with heartfelt words that will move the dispute toward real and lasting peace. If you do, He promises to give you a mysterious peace that will calm your heart and even your mind, allowing you a respite from pounding thoughts that awaken you in the wee hours of the morning.

You are never guaranteed peace with your adversary. That kind of peace takes two. But you are guaranteed "the peace of God." He will give you His presence and His peace—a sense that whatever happens He will take care of you and use the situation for His purposes. You will survive and even thrive, if you trust Him and do what He asks.

Focus on the positive

> Finally, brothers and sisters, whatever is true, whatever is
> worthy of respect, whatever is just, whatever is pure, what-
> ever is lovely, whatever is commendable, if something is ex-
> cellent or praiseworthy, think about these things.
> —Philippians 4:8

In my darkest season of conflict, God gave good gifts. He brought unexpected friends with words of encouragement at just the right times, even when they did not know about the dispute. Timely songs on the radio offered hope. Serendipitous gifts showed up in my mailbox to cheer me after a particularly difficult bout. One friend laminated and framed a psalm that echoed what I was feeling and propelled me to the same Source of comfort. She did not know about the dispute either.

Commendable men, worthy of respect, led negotiations that were excruciating but fair, just, and kind. I am grateful. An excellent female counselor walked with me. My husband offered solid support throughout the ordeal. A woman leader, upon hearing about the situation, later opened a door for a new and exciting ministry opportunity. And, of course, there are the lessons I enumerated earlier. Faith is tested in conflict but God brings many surprising glimpses of sunshine, if we will only see them. Focus on the positive gifts that God provides along the way—messages that He is with you and will carry you through to the other side.

Emulate God's role models

> And what you learned and received and heard and saw in me,
> do these things. And the God of peace will be with you.
> —Philippians 4:9

In the Bible we observe men and women who model how to respond to conflict God's way. Paul includes himself in this austere company, and for good reason, as we saw in Chapter One. He endured a barrage of personal attacks and difficult people. He had run-ins with Peter, the Jews, and even other Christians. Not only was he verbally assaulted but he was physically beaten, stoned, and whipped—an extreme most of us will never experience, praise God! Yet he responded God's way. God asks us to do the same.

Sisters, despite the tough disputes that you will face if you choose to serve God, you can choose to bravely walk through conflict God's way. We hope that the insights and strategies we have supplied in these pages will help. We pray that you will walk away from the controversy arm in arm with your adversary, but regardless, you *can* walk away stronger, wiser, and more seasoned to serve our great God. You can honor Him in the process, show others what He alone can do, and bring Him glory! And that's the bottom line. Do well, my sisters.

The LORD bless you and protect you;
The LORD make his face to shine upon you, and be gracious to you;
the LORD lift up his countenance upon you and give you peace.

—Numbers 6:24–26

Bibliography

Aikman, David, "Attack Dogs of Christendom," *Christianity Today*, August 2007.

Allender, Dan, and Tremper Longman, *Bold Love*. Colorado Springs, CO: NavPress, 1992.

Barash, Susan, *Tripping the Prom Queen*. New York: St. Martin's Press, 2006.

Belenky, Mary, Blythe Clinchy, Nancy Goldberger, Jill Tarule. *Women's Ways of Knowing*. New York: Basic Books by Harper Collins, 1986.

Bendel, Mary-Ann, "TV's Super-Woman," *Ladies Home Journal*, March 1988.

Bisagno, John, *God Is*. Wheaton, IL: Victor Books, 1983.

Braiker, Harriet, *The Disease to Please*. New York: McGraw-Hill, 2001.

Briles, Judith, *Women to Women 2000: Becoming Sabotage Saavy in the New Millennium*. New Horizon Press, 1999.

Brown, Lyn Mikel, *Girlfighting*. New York: New York University Press, 2003.

Chesler, Phyllis, *Woman's Inhumanity to Woman*. New York: Thunder's Mouth Press/Nation Books, 2001.

de Spinoza, Benedict, *A Theological-Political Treatise and a Political Treatise*, trans. R. H. M. Elwes, 1883; reprint ed., New York, NY: Dover Publications, 1951.

Driscoll, Richard, "Will Women Be Better Managers? Gender Conflict at Work," *Transitions, The Journal of Men's Perspectives*, 1999.

Dudley, Carl S., "Conflict: Synonym for Congregation," www.fact.hartsem.edu/topfindings/topicalfinding_article3.htm

Dwyer, Carol, and Linda Johnson, *Grades, Accomplishments, and Correlates: Gender and Fair Assessment*. ed. Warren Willingham and Nancy Cole. Mahwah, NJ: Erlbaum, 1997.

Fiorina, Carly, *Tough Choices, A Memoir*. New York, NY: Penguin Books, 2006.

Frame, John M., *Evangelical Reunion*. Grand Rapids, MI: Baker, 1991.

Gangel, Kenneth, and Samuel Canine, *Communication and Conflict Management in Churches and Christian Organizations*. Eugene, Oregon: Wipf and Stock Publishers, 2002.

Garbarino, James, *See Jane Hit: Why Girls Are Growing More Violent and What We Can Do About It*. New York: Penguin Books, 2006.

Gilligan, Carol, *In a Different Voice*. Cambridge, Mass: Harvard University Press, 1982.

Goodwin, Marjorie Harness, and Charles Goodwin, "Children's Arguing," in *Language, Gender, and Sex in Comparative Perspectives*, ed. Susan U. Phillips, Susan Steele, and Christine Tanz, Cambridge: Cambridge University Press, 1987.

Heim, Pat and Susan Murphy, *In the Company of Women: Indirect Aggression Among Women, Why We Hurt Each Other and How to Stop*. New York: Jeremy P. Tarcher/Putnam, 2001.

Hoff Summers, Christian, "The Problem with American Feminists," *Dallas Morning News*, June 17, 2007.

Hubbard, M. Gay, "Women, The Misunderstood Majority," *Contemporary Christian Counseling*. Gary R. Collins, General Editor, Word publishing, 1992.

Johnson, David W., *Human Relations and Your Career: A Guide to Interpersonal Skills*. Englewood Cliffs: Prentice-Hall, 1978.

Kerber, Lisa, and Rand Harris, *Substance Abuse Among Female Inmates*. Texas Department of Criminal Justice, Institutional Division, 1998.

LaRue, John C., "Forced Exits: A Too-Common Ministry Hazard," *Your Church*, Mar/Apr 1996.

Lever, Janet, "Sex Differences in the Complexity of Children's Play And Games," *American Sociological Review*, Vol. 43, 1978.

Levin, Phyllis Lee, *Abigail Adams, A Biography*. New York: Ballantine Books, 1987.

Maxwell, John, *Winning With People*. Nashville: Thomas Nelson, 2004.

————, "Velvet-Covered Bricks," *Leadership Wired*, August 2007, Volume 10, Issue 12.

Pachter, Barbara, and Susan McGee, *The Power of Positive Confrontation*. New York, NY: Marlowe & Company, 2000.

Pink, Arthur, *The Attributes of God*. Grand Rapids, MI: Baker Book House, 1975, 78.

Priolo, Lou, *Pleasing People*. Phillipsburg, NJ: P&R Publishing, 2007.

Robinson, Duke, *Too Nice For Your Own Good*. New York: Time Warner Books, 1997.

Rubin, Jeffrey, and Bert Brown, *The Social Psychology of Bargaining and Negotiating*. New York: Academic Press, 1975.

Sande, Ken, *Strike the Shepherd; Losing Pastors in the Church*. www.peacemaker.net, key articles, December 2007.

Sax, Leonard, *Why Gender Matters.* New York, Broadway Books, 2005.

Shelley, Marshall, *Well-Intentioned Dragons: Ministering to Problem People in the Church.* Minneapolis, MN: Bethany House Publishers, 1985.

Stone, Douglas, Bruce Patton, and Sheila Heen, *Difficult Conversations.* New York, NY: Penguin Books, 1999.

Strauss, Richard L., *The Joy of Knowing God.* Neptune, NJ: Loizeaux Brothers, 1984.

Notes

Introduction

1. LaRue, "Forced Exits," 72.
2. Dudley, "Conflict: Synonym for Congregation."
3. Focus on the Family, 1998.
4. Ken Sande, (Keynote Address) "Executives Who Resolve Conflict Biblically," XP-Seminar, February 5, 2008, Dallas, Texas.

Chapter One

1. September 5, 2007, in a chapel message *How to Stand Strong in Stressful Times* at Dallas Theological Seminary, Dallas, Texas. (http://www.dts.edu/media/podcasts/archives)
2. Mark 2:8.
3. Acts 9:20–30.
4. "Judaizers" refers to Jewish Christians who sought to induce Gentiles to observe Jewish religious customs: to "judaize." It appears that these individuals agreed with much of the apostolic kerygma but sought to regulate the admission of Gentiles into the covenant people of God through circumcision and the keeping of the ceremonial law. (*Evangelical Dictionary of Theology*, 2nd Ed., 2001.)
5. Philippians 1:15.
6. Philippians 1:17.

7. Philippians 4:2–3 (NIV).

8. Levin, *Abigail Adams.*

9. Ibid., 84.

10. Ibid., 424.

11. Ibid., 426, 427.

12. Ibid., 468, 469.

13. Driscoll, "Will Women Be Better Managers? Gender Conflict at Work," 19.

14. Briles, *Women to Women 2000.*

15. Heim and Murphy, *In the Company of Women,* 1.

16. Ibid., 9.

17. Maxwell, *Winning With People,* 210, 211.

18. Heim and Murphy, *In the Company of Women,* 54.

19. Sax, *Why Gender Matters,* 85.

20. Brown, *Girlfighting,* 180.

21. Garbarino, *See Jane Hit,* 3.

22. Ibid., 3, 4.

23. Ibid., 4.

24. Dwyer and Johnson, *Grades, Accomplishments, and Correlates,* 127–56.

25. *Balancing the Equation: Where Are Women and Girls in Science, Engineering, and Technology?* National Council for Research on Women monograph, 2001. Press release online at www.ncrw.org/research/scipress.htm.

26. Heim and Murphy, *In the Company of Women,* 36, 37.

27. Chesler, *Woman's Inhumanity to Women,* 24.

Chapter Two

1. Chesler, *Woman's Inhumanity to Women,* 1. See also page 16 where a high profile feminist editor refused to look at the manuscript.

2. Hoff Summers, "The Problem with American Feminists."

3. Hubbard, "Women, The Misunderstood Majority," 98, 99.

4. Sax, *Why Gender Matters,* 58.

5. Goodwin and Goodwin, "Children's Arguing," 200–48.

6. Chesler, *Woman's Inhumanity to Woman,* 2, 3.

7. Ibid., 6.

8. Heim and Murphy, *In the Company of Women,* 6, 7.

9. Gilligan, *In a Different Voice,* 24–63.

10. Ibid.

11. Heim and Murphy, *In The Company of Women,* 88, 89.

12. Lever, "Sex Differences in the Complexity of Children's Play And Games," 471–483.

13. Barash, *Tripping the Prom Queen*, 32, 33.

14. Ibid., 6, 7.

15. Ibid., 166, 167.

16. Ibid., 172.

17. Heim and Murphy, *In the Company of Women*, introductory page.

Chapter Three

1. Eva Kor's story is depicted in a film by Bob Hercules and Cheri Pugh entitled *Forgiving Dr. Mengele*. The film won the Special Jury Prize for Best Documentary at the Slamdance Film Festival in 2006.

2. Shelley, *Well-Intentioned Dragons*, 35.

3. Stone, Patton, and Heen, *Difficult Conversations*, 14.

4. Ibid., 112.

5. Ibid., 114.

6. Priolo, *Pleasing People*, 18.

7. Braiker, *The Disease to Please*, 11.

8. Priolo, *Pleasing People*, 39.

9. Ibid., 22-25.

10. Braiker, *The Disease to Please*, 33.

11. Ibid.

12. Robinson, *Too Nice For Your Own Good*, 31, 32.

13. Bendel, "TV's Super-Woman," 170.

14. Robinson, *Too Nice For Your Own Good*, 1.

15. Priolo, *Pleasing People*, 31.

16. Fiorina, *Tough Choices*, 70.

17. Ibid., 95.

18. Maxwell, "Velvet-Covered Bricks" (www.injoy.com/newsletters/leadership).

Chapter Four

1. Aikman, "Attack Dogs of Christendom," 52.

2. The term "dragon" comes from Marshall Shelley's book entitled *Well-Intentioned Dragons, Ministering to Problem People in the Church*, (Minneapolis, MN: Bethany House Publishers, 1985). This book is an excellent resource for men.

3. Dan Reiland, *The Pastor's Coach*, Church Politics, Part 1, 1, 2 (Church_Politics.html).

4. Pachter and McGee, *The Power of Positive Confrontation*, 56.

5. Fiorina, *Tough Choices*, 106.

6. de Spinoza, *A Theological-Political Treatise and a Political Treatise*, 6.

7. Shelley, *Well-Intentioned Dragons*, 43.

8. Ibid., 45, 46.

9. Ibid., 47.

10. Belenky, Clinchy, Goldberger, and Tarule, *Women's Ways of Knowing*.

11. Galatians 5:20–21 (NIV).

Chapter Five

1. CBS 11 News, July 5, 2007, http://cbs11tv.com/topstories/localstory 186183018.html. This incident occurred at the Creekpoint Apartments in Dallas, Texas.

2. This story was reported in *The Week* magazine, October 12, 2007, page 4.

3. Ibid.

4. Johnson, *Human Relations and Your Career*, 247.

5. Stone, Patton, and Heen, *Difficult Conversations*, 46, 47.

6. Ibid., 48.

Chapter Six

1. Luke 1:37.

2. Larry Crabb, in the Foreword to *Bold Love* by Allender and Longman, 12.

3. The NET Bible, page 1694, note 2sn.

4. Paul was quoting Proverbs 25:21, 22 in verse 20.

5. NET Bible note number 4, page 1089.

6. Pink, *The Attributes of God*, 78.

7. Strauss, *The Joy of Knowing God*, 157.

8. Bisagno, *God Is*, 21.

9. Allender and Longman, *Bold Love*, 17.

10. Dennis Johnson, "Peacemakers," appendix in Frame's *Evangelical Reunion*, 171.

11. Allender and Longman, *Bold Love*, 37.

12. Ibid., 229-309. For an interesting and more in-depth study of this topic, we suggest you read these chapters.

13. Ibid., 287, 298.

14. Kerber and Harris, *Substance Abuse Among Female Inmates*, 2.

15. Ibid., 233.

Chapter Seven

1. FoxNews.com (February 6, 2006). Story concept by Sam O'Neal, St. Charles, Illinois, *Leadership Journal*, Summer 2006, Vol. XXVII, Number 3, page 69.

2. Stone, Patton, and Heen, *Difficult Conversations*, 16,17.

3. NET Bible translator's note 36 (page 1070).

4. NET Bible note 36, quote by W. McKane (page 1070).

5. Rubin and Brown, *The Social Psychology of Bargaining and Negotiating*, 64.

6. Gangel and Canine, *Communication and Conflict Management in Churches and Christian Organizations*, 216.

Chapter Eight

1. This section stems from a helpful interview with Steve Roese, executive pastor of Irving Bible Church, Irving, Texas, with Sue Edwards on December 19, 2007.

2. Shelley, *Well-Intentioned Dragons*, 67.

3. Ibid., 44.

4. Ibid., 67.

5. Ecclesiastes 4:9–12.

Chapter Nine

1. Stone, Patton, and Heen, *Difficult Conversations*, 15–17.

2. Ibid., 16. For specifics on effective conversation strategies, read the entire book. Although the spiritual dimension is missing, they have written an invaluable guide to sorting through the varied levels of conflict. We recommend this book for both men and women.

3. This book was published by Bethany House Publishers, Minneapolis, Minnesota, 1985.

4. From an interview on December 19, 2007.

5. This study can be found at http://www.cnn.com/2007/LIVING/work-life/08/02/angry.men.women.reut/index.html

6. Sande, *Strike the Shepherd, Losing Pastors in the Church*, (www.peacemaker.net).

7. http://www.dts.edu/departments/campus/ccl/

Epilogue

1. www.crosswalk.com/movies, January 1, 2008.

LEADING WOMEN TO
THE HEART OF GOD

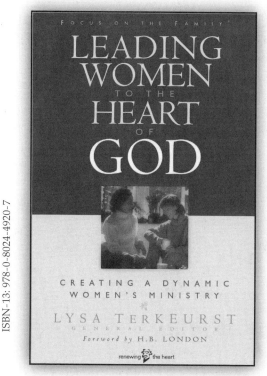

ISBN-13: 978-0-8024-4920-7

Building a vibrant, God-honoring women's ministry is an enormous challenge. *Leading Women to the Heart of God* is a comprehensive compilation of articles by leading Christian women, addressing key areas of women's ministry. Anyone involved in women's ministry must have a copy of this unique handbook!

1-800-678-8812 · MOODYPUBLISHERS.COM

TRANSFORMING TOGETHER

Transforming Together presents the model for genuine spiritual mentoring through the power and work of Christ in the lives of women faithfully pouring into one another.

MOODY
PUBLISHERS.

1-800-678-8812 · MOODYPUBLISHERS.COM